FRAGRANT FLOWERS AT THE FEET OF MY FLAMBOYANT FLUTIST
(DEVOTIONAL POEMS TO KRISHNA)

JYOTI ATUL BHATT

Copyright © 2022 Jyoti Atul Bhatt

This is a work of poetry. The author asserts her moral right to be identified as the owner of her intellectual property.
All Rights Reserved

First Edition: April 2022
Printed in India

Printed at PrintOne Graphics, Navi Mumbai.
Typeset in Adobe Garamond Pro

ISBN: 978-93-92661-81-5

Cover Design: Prashant Gurav

STORYMIRROR
Stories that reflect you

Publisher:	StoryMirror Infotech Pvt. Ltd.
	145, First Floor, Powai Plaza, Hiranandani Gardens, Powai, Mumbai - 400076, India

Web:	https://storymirror.com
Facebook:	https://facebook.com/storymirror
Twitter:	https://twitter.com/story_mirror
Instagram:	https://instagram.com/storymirror
Email:	marketing@storymirror.com

No part of this book may be reproduced, or stored in a retrieval system, or transmitted in any form or by any means, electronic, mechanical, photocopying, recording, or otherwise, without express written permission of the publisher.

DEDICATION

I HUMBLY OFFER THESE

FRAGRANT FLOWERS
AT THE FEET OF MY FLAMBOYANT FLUTIST

SHRI SHRI RADHA SHARADBIHARI

ACKNOWLEDGEMENTS

The accomplishment of this book would have been impossible without the grace of Shri Radha Sharadbihari …..my eternal thanks to them. I will remain forever indebted to Srila Bhaktivedanta Swami Srila Prabhupada who brought me closer to Krishna. The Bhagvad Gita sloka translations used in a few poems have been taken from Prabhupadaji's translation from the book 'Bhagvad Gita As It Is.' My sincere thanks to Shri Radha Govind Maharaj, for the knowledge that I have received from him. My heartfelt gratitude to Shri Bhaiji, Shri Dilip Kumar Roy, Gurumayi Swami Chidvilasananda, who have been a significant inspiration in my devotional services to Krishna. My humble homage to all the great saints who have touched my life in several ways.

My heartfelt thanks to my dear loving father, late Shri Bhaskar R. Dave, who would have shed tears of joy on seeing this book, and my dear mother for the sanskars she inculcated in me. Many thanks to my elder sister, Dr. Nita Aditya Jain, for writing an absolutely heart touching foreword to this book and for always encouraging me. I thank her from the bottom of my heart for her kind words; I don't deserve the praise she has showered on me so profusely. I thank my younger sister, Dr. Amishi Deepak Arora, for her constant encouragement and her good wishes. I thank my late father-in-law, Shri Mohanlal Bhatt, and my late mother-in-law, Smt. Kundanben Bhatt, for their blessings. I also thank my well-wishers, late Shri Bharatbhai Pandya, late Smt. Sushilaben Pandya, Shri Himanshubhai Bhatt, Smt. Vibhaben Bhatt and Smt. Harshaben Shah. I thank my dear husband, Atul Bhatt, for his great support and encouragement. I am also extremely grateful to my daughters, Janitri, her husband Pranav Pandya, Rudrika and her husband Alok Bhatt for their encouragement and good wishes. For every poem I sent to Rudrika, she would invariably respond enthusiastically with a beautiful comment that never failed to bolster my morale, motivating me to publish this piece of work. A last word of thanks to my dear grandchildren, Krishna, Ruchira and Advait for listening with zeal to the lilas of Krishna.

A FEW WORDS

My Flutist has played His flute again…… magically mesmerising my mind, maneuvering it to do as He desires. He has used my hand once again to write with His versatile pen and the poems are nothing but a manifestation of His inspiration and His ingenuity!

'Fragrant flowers at the feet of my Flamboyant Flutist (devotional poems to Krishna) is a sequel to my first book titled, 'How Krishna Came Into Their Lives' which comprised of only a handful of poems within a section 'The author's own poems'. Some readers kept goading me to publish some more. With the sole purpose of encouraging and inspiring fellow wayfarers on the same spiritual path, I decided to make this humble offering.

Sincere souls who are seriously seeking the Ultimate Absolute Truth, who are longing to leave the labyrinth of lesser laurels of this earth and desperately desiring God Realization might be able to relate to my reflections and struggles on my journey that I am still traversing. Hopefully these words may strike a cord and some new avenues for a few. Even if one soul finds a meaningful companion inside the pages of this book, I shall be eternally grateful for the opportunity to have rendered a trivial service to my Flutist.

My flamboyant Flutist needs no introduction and I'm sure you must have guessed who I am referring to; no other divine forms are associated with the flute as Lord Shri Krishna is. It was His much loved, highly esteemed and most legendary flute that earned Him popular names such as Murlidhar, Bansidhar and so on. If you want to know someone who is a complete embodiment of nothing but unconditional love, compassion, mercy and all the admirable adjectives that describe perfection then try to know Lord Shri Krishna …..the one and only! He is that unique Personality of Godhead who would willingly submit to your rebuke and reprimand if you lovingly considered Him to be your own child. He would love to be taunted and teased if you lovingly considered Him to be your dear friend. He would lovingly reciprocate to your passionate cries as He did to Mira who loved Him and looked upon Him as her true husband and to the gopis of Vrindavan who lovingly worshipped Him as their divine paramour! Informal and intimate dealings with Him as if He is one's very own please Him much more than Vedic stutis and heavenly hymns of praise.

Life has been a see-saw, sometimes going up and sometimes down, sometimes experiencing excruciating pain in body and mind and sometimes heavenly happiness. But behind the mundane melodrama there has always been one steady force though imperceptible, intangible and inconceivable……the power of His immeasurable mercy and love that has steered me through the dark waters and navigated the thoughts of my mind to understand that every dark day only got me closer to His light and as I slowly inch my way up to Him I trust that He will one day extend His adorable arm to pull me into His kingdom of everlasting love and peace! In my deepest gratitude to my dearest One…..my Lord of Lords I submissively offer a few fragrant flowers of love at His lovely lotus feet!

FOREWORD

To be asked to write a Foreword for your sister's collection of poems by the poet herself is a mighty big responsibility that needs to be justified verifiably. And above all, my greatest Honour and privilege.

The transition of a brilliant multifaceted daughter, wife, mother and professor into a spiritually inclined champion of devotion has been an incredible one. From being a freelance writer to becoming the Director of the Indological Research Centre, Gurudev Siddha Peeth, Ganeshpuri, guiding research in religion and spirituality to receiving the most delectable accolades for her book 'How Krishna Came into their Lives', Jyoti Bhatt's journey has been an uphill path in spiritual enrichment and realization. And as 'from hour to hour we ripe and ripe', so has Jyoti Bhatt moved with time, from learning to knowing, and culminating in an awakening of her 'love'; and thereby hangs the tale of Jyoti Bhatt's surrender to the Object of her love.

Jyoti Bhatt's anthology, 'Fragrant Flowers at the Feet of my Flamboyant Flutist', is a soulful accumulation of the poet's expressions in monologues with her faith and of her faith over a period of time. On reading the first few and then gradually the rest of the poems, one is amazed at Jyoti's singular focus and rendezvous with 'Krishna'. The poems take us along a virtual trip that subtly awakens our existential beings which fortunately, we as readers, get to encounter first hand! Each poem unfolds the dust of ignorance and ignominy that we wrap around ourselves in the journey of life: but we are made to turn around as she skilfully succeeds in drawing us slowly and slowly, closer and closer to our own faith! We begin to see her passion, we begin to feel the intensity of her assurance of the presence of her faith and ultimately she succeeds in convincing even the non-believers. That is Jyoti Bhatt, the eloquent admirer and devotee of Krishna!

The ease with which Jyoti gives way to powerful expression is outstanding and it is without doubt that love alone can win Him. The aptly chosen titles of her poems urge the readers to look for more, to unravel the ultimate truth of the universe just as the rose reveals its ultimate beauty when its petals gradually open and reveal the truth of creation. In the poem- You are Everywhere she shares her firm and well learned belief that Krishna is 'far away and yet nearer than the nearest both within and without. Objectifying the man of the material world the 'Jiva',' that heaps unwanted karmas, is asked to pause, think and know that God is Everywhere! Heap on heap and load over load of doubts makes the myriad minded man swing like a pendulum in delirium, but unwavering faith comes to the believer's rescue that 'Only Parthsarathi Krishna could do so!'. The poet in total surrender has advised to put the ego away to be able to see the unseen and know the unknown. The poems are an epitome of the glasslike transparency of her simple faith in her passionate affair with her Flutist!

Justly, Jyoti Bhatt's Anthology weaves reality with vision. The grace of her exquisite diction adds a spark and a sparkle to her expressions which cascade down our mind's eye with effortless ease inspiring trust in her Lover.

A collection that will enthral all hearts and touch both the believer and the non-believer!

All in all, a great read!

Wishing Jyoti Bhatt several awakenings in knowledge throughout her journey of life!

Nita (Dave) Jain, PGCTE, PhD.

Faculty at ICAI

Formerly Dean(2016-17), Faculty of Arts,

Principal (Retd.) and HOD (Retd)

Christ Church College,

Formerly Convener, Board of Studies(English),

CSJM University,

Kanpur, India

Contents

1. Pilgrimage To The Heart	17
2. There Is No One Like Krishna	19
3. I Ness.....Ahamta	22
4. The Only Way	24
5. Beauty Personified	26
6. The Nectar Of Your Name	28
7. A Teardrop Of Love	30
8. Self Will And God's Will	32
9. Ultimately It's Your Will That Prevails	35
10. Humility	39
11. Expropriate My Heart	41

12. When And Why?	43
13. Let Me Tune In To Your Will	45
14. Remembering You	47
15. What Need I Fear	49
16. Player Of Players	51
17. A Persistent Longing	52
18. Shame On Me	54
19. Pure Love	56
20. I Pause To Ponder	59
21. Open-Eyed Slumber	62
22. I Am Incapable	64
23. Incredible Creation	66
24. God Cannot Walk For Me	68
25. Radha	70
26. On Death	72
27. Dispel My Distressing Doubts	75
28. The Elixir Of Love	77
29. A Heavy Heartache	79
30. Leave Me To Lead Myself On	81
31. My One And Only	83
32. The Heart Is Your Holy Haven	85
33. You Are Everywhere	87
34. Time	89

35. Your Promise	91
36. When Will My Heart Assume Radha's Golden Glow Of Love	93
37. Why Do I Hurt You Again And Again	95
38. Practising The Presence Of God	97
39. Who Am I?	99
40. A Plea To Patit Paavan Krishna	101
41. Pain Comes As Mercy To Devotees	103
42. Negativity Too Has A Place In Your Divine Drama	106
43. Your Hidden Hand	108
44. O My Mind	110
45. Prayers	112
46. Juxtaposition	114
47. True Dharma	117
48. Faith	120
49. The Secret Key	122
50. Painful Love	125
51. Like A River To The Sea, Let Me Just Flow To You	127
52. Searching The Unsearchable	129
53. The Time Is Now	132
54. How?	134
Glossary	137

1. PILGRIMAGE TO THE HEART

Retiring to the holy Himalayas
or residing in the venerated Vrindavandham,
leaving the vile world behind
appeared to be an alluring idea
an appropriate one indeed
to find You and focus on You
O Krishna.

But when You graciously kindled
a lamp in my heart
I realized in its luminous light
that You live in hearts
as You say so in the Bhagvad Gita:
'īshvarah sarva-bhūtānām hrid-deśhe 'rjuna tishthati';
then why not create Vrindavandham within
or bring the silence and serenity
of the Himalayas
within my mundane self.

The obstacles I assume
are just concoctions of the mind.
The real hurdles blocking the path

are *kaam* (lust), *krodh* (anger), *lobh* (greed),
moha (attachment), *matsar* (ego)
which follow me wherever I go.

The pilgrimage to the heart
is what I need to embark on.
Let me turn my focus from
the outward into the inward,
from the ephemeral to the ethereal,
from the transient to the transcendental.
The true temple is within
where You have always
remained enshrined
waiting to be worshipped,
to love and be loved!

2. THERE IS NO ONE LIKE KRISHNA

There is no one like Krishna
and there never will be
either in this world, or in any other *loka*!

He gives Himself in totality
without holding back an iota
for He is a laudable lover of love
and love alone can win Him!

Where will one find
a master serving His servant?
Where will one find
God serving His devotee?
Where will one find
the Lord of Lords
becoming a humble beggar of love?

At the end of a tiresome day
when warrior Arjun slept
soundly and insouciantly .....
Who kept awake to serve his tired horses?
Who else other than *Parthsarathi* Krishna
can credibly do so!

In the festival at King Yudhisthira's court
which king has ever served the guests
by picking up their plates after they had eaten?
Only *Tribhuvanpati* Krishna could do so!

When Mother Yashoda scolded,
reprimanded and even punished Him
Who allowed Himself to be tied up
even though He was *Mukunda*
the giver of liberation?
Only Krishna could do so!

For a few drops of buttermilk
who would dance to the tunes of the gopis
even though He was *Sarvaloka maheshvaram*?
Only Krishna could do so!

Who didn't hesitate for a second to
wash His friend Sudama's feet
even though He was *Dwarkadheesh*?
Only Krishna could do so!

Who would ever give up *Chappanbhog*
to eat banana peels
given by Vidurani overawed with love
and devotion for Him

When he was *Jaganath Himself*
Only Krishna could do so!

Who willingly became a lowly loser
in games that He played with His childhood friends
even though He was *Achyuta*?
Only Krishna could do so!

Who would disguise Himself in
a million different ways and
go through endless hardships
and even ask Radharani
to put her foot on His head
just to get His beloved's sidelong glance
even though He was *Radhanath*?
Only Krishna could do so!

Oh Krishna there IS no one like You
and there never will be!

3. I NESS....AHAMTA

I ness...*ahamta*
is the only wall that separates
me from You
which though gossamer like
has the strength of iron……..

If for a moment
I ponder on this principle
I come to realize
that it is absolutely impossible
for me to break it,
any amount of my enormous efforts
will ultimately be anaemic.

Dissolution and disintegration
of I ness would mean
existence in a state of nonexistence
being in a state of not being.
Forgetting that I am
a wife, a mother, a child, a sibling.
Forgetting that I am a Hindu,
a Brahmin, a Vaishnav,

good, bad or any other differentiation
that goes with a person.

Becoming oblivious of all that matters
or doesn't matter in this
mundane materialism......
dissolving the dumbest desire
dwelling in my depths,
rising above likes, dislikes,
wants and needs......
remaining rock steady and unruffled
in praise and blame,
honor and dishonor,
success and failure,
heat and cold.

O make me
a mindless monkey
moved, motivated and maneuvered
only by You, my Merciful *Madhav!*

4. THE ONLY WAY

O Krishna
Even though I can experience You
as an embodiment of love,
a manifestation of mercy,
a personification of beauty…..but yet
my perception fails to witness You,
my words fail to portray You……
and my emotions fail to declare
the inexplicable experience of love.

No shastras have yet shown me
the surest signboard pointing at You.
No path has yet been the perfect
and precise way towards You.

Techniques to transfer to the transcendental
tried and tested……
secrets of spiritual practices
searched and scanned……
efforts eventually meeting
dead ends.

Nothing can attract the All Attractive,
nothing can please Pleasure Personified,
and nothing can be given
to the one and only Giver of everything
save love....

The one and only way
I realize now is to
love You as I would love my own self
with soulful simplicity of heart…...
with love that is pure and unadulterated,
unquestioning, indubitable and unconditional,
without any expectations of anything at all
and without any explanations
for anything at all!

5. BEAUTY PERSONIFIED

Oh beautiful blue boy Krishna
Your blissful beauty
grows on me day by day....
Your ever entrancing eyes
invite me to delve into their depths
......a wondrous world
which need wings of surrender
to fathom.

Your rosy lips fortified into
a spellbinding smile
send sweet shivers
down my spine.

Your captivating curly hair
adorned with a crown of peacock feathers
enchants me as I experience
inexplicable ecstasy.

Your heavenly hands
holding the fetching flute
and Your lovely lotus feet.....

make my eyes want to
endlessly ogle at You!

If Your *archa vigraha* can be
so engaging and exotic
what must Your actual
spiritual form be
and what would be the experience
of beholding beauty personified
is just beyond my ken.

Oh if the camera of my eyes
could capture
Your charming charismatic countenance
and pin it permanently
on the wall of my mind
my heart would surely soar
to the zenith of a zillionaire!

6. THE NECTAR OF YOUR NAME

O Krishna
You have been
waiting and waiting for me
to open my heart to You.
I listlessly let my lifetimes pass by
without bothering to peek out
of the little window.

The dust and din of the world outside
went hammer and tong
to make me deaf to the inner call.
I made no attempts to hear You
nor did I ever bother to seek You.

Now when this realization rankles my rudiments....
I want to warmly welcome You in
But the house of my heart
is choc-a-block with crazy concepts
and *karmic* knots.....
laden with layers of dust.
Only the nectar of Your Name

can nutritiously nurture me
and purify me.

O my heart .....my soul
and every atom of my anatomy
please give yourself lovingly,
large-heartedly and longingly to Krishna.

O my mind
take a well-deserved vacation from the world
and get ravenous to enjoy in the
royal resort of *Naam Bhagvan*.

O my ego
please leave me alone for a while
and stop patting my back
and making me think
how devout is my devotion.

I yearn to be all alone in
the sanctity of the Supersoul.
Let me melt into the magnitude
of the magnificent moments
of mindful meditation on You!

❀❀❀❀✸❀❀❀❀

7. A TEARDROP OF LOVE

All You want Krishna
is a crystal clear teardrop of love
love that is *ananya*
that in deep and clear understanding
knows no other, sees no other
and hears no other.

A teardrop of love
replete with reminisces
of all the mountains of mercy
repeatedly received from You.

A teardrop of love
brimming with gratitude
for all the bountiful blessings
bestowed.

A teardrop of love
filled with a firm unflinching faith
that You are my fast friend forever
and my warmest well wisher
-a fantastic Ferryman

who will unequivocally ferry me across
this fierce ocean of illusion and free me
from the fool's paradise I am floating in.

O Krishna
as I stand at the shore
let me give myself completely
to this little teardrop and wait
for the waves
of Your endless ocean of love
to sweep me up to You one day!

8. SELF WILL AND GOD'S WILL

I covetously crave to be released
from my *karmic* creations
and their reactions
that have anchored me since aeons
bringing me back life after life and
immobilizing me from moving on
to the Lord of my heart!

Realization has finally dawned now
that the cunning culprit is
my self centered will
which has always driven my mind
and maneuvered its musings.

Dire desire dwelling deep
taught this culprit
to do its bidding.....
and one mundane desire
dwindled into millions
which in turn multiplied
mushrooming into trillions
and caught my soul
in its self created *karmic* web.

if only this self will turns forever
to the Lord of my heart …..
merging and melting into
His Supreme Will,
forgetting its insignificant identity
and renouncing the fruits
of its every thought, word and deed
only then will I never be entangled again
in the labyrinth of the lower laurels.

Negligent and nonchalant
this self will has invited reactions
that have fettered my feet
with an unflinching firmness.

Oh when will this self will
disperse all these damaging desires
and dovetail itself to the Will
of the Lord of my heart
and learn to dance
to the tunes of His flute's call.

When my proud self will
become a docile dog
loyally licking His Tender Feet
my mind will then be equipoised

in success and failure,
happiness and unhappiness.

When His Supreme Will alone prevails
and I accept it with equanimity
all the iron chains that have bound me
will be broken
and I will forever be free to fly
to the land of my Lord for eternity!

9. ULTIMATELY IT'S YOUR WILL THAT PREVAILS

When my aim is not achieved,
a target not touched
or a desired destination not reached
.....when happenings don't unfold
according to the plans
of my mind or
when the results of an action
are contrary to my anticipation
I fret and fume
and fear to face the formidable.

The restless mind then begins
to analyze aimlessly
whirling around could haves
and should haves
vainly wishing
my thoughts, words or actions
were more congruous
with my expectations.

But amazing is Your mercy
Your grace....Your kindness
and Your benevolent eye
upon my little self ....Krishna
that makes me realize
and understand
with concrete conviction
that whatever happens
happens because it has to happen.

The wise say
that even the tiniest of leaves
cannot move without Your Will.
Material nature is Your energy
totally tuned in to Your thoughts....
moving each and every living creature
in the direction You would want it to
for its own welfare and growth.

You are the ultimate cause
of all causes and
as You say in the Gita
"Ishvarah sarva-bhutanam
Hrd-dese 'juna tisthati
Bhramayam sarva bhutani

Yantrarudhani mayaya"

Meaning:

"The Supreme Lord is situated in everyone's heart, O Arjuna, and is directing the wanderings of all living entities, who are seated as on a machine, made of the material energy."

So when the remote control
to move the machine of my body
lies in Your Hands.....
and I am but a puppet
whose strings are being pulled by You
why should I ever worry, regret
or feel remorseful?

All that lies in my hands.... I understand
is having a definite desire
to annihilate my senseless self will
and let it merge
into Your Supreme Will.
My happiness lies only
in Your happiness.

I pray from the bottom
of my heart that I keep
my mind machine

Fragrant Flowers At The Feet Of My Flamboyant Flutist.

well-oiled and smoothly functioning
by *smaran* (remembrance)
and *manan* (contemplation)
which alone can dovetail it
to do as You desire.....
Let my system revel in....the fact that
ultimately it is Your Will alone that prevails!

10. HUMILITY

O Chaitanya Mahaprabhu
I humbly beg of You
to let so much humility
seep into every subtle cell
of myself
that it silences my *ahankar* (ego)
and soaks my stupid mind
in its heavenly hues and colors.....
repeatedly reminding myself
that **'me'** is but a minute minuscule
and **'mine'** is just
a misunderstanding of the mind.

That I am but an insignificant instrument
that exists only to play the tune
that pampers and pleases You.

Let me pursue Your plan
and perceive perfection
in all that destiny drives to my door
and accept all the activities

it asks me to execute
and accomplish the aim ascertained by You.

I seek to dissolve my self will
into Your Supreme Will
so that my small self
serves You selflessly and silently!

11. EXPROPRIATE MY HEART

O Krishna
When will I burn
in the fire of separation?
When will my dry eyes
be welled with tears
pleading out in passionate pain?
When will I experience excruciating
pining pangs for You?

Every day goes by
with me eating, sleeping
and merrily indulging
in worldly ways.
I clamorously claim
that You are
my heart and soul
the axis of my life....
but these words seem empty
when I continue to exist
like a lifeless being
without a heart and soul.

O Krishna
I have realized that
no amount of self effort
will bring me to Your Feet....
For You are not located
at a fixed spot
where one can just walk up to.
You can only be reached
if You want us to reach You.

So kindly come,
expropriate my heart
and annex my mind.
Only then will my thoughts
vainly wandering into the world
be forever deposed and overthrown
and my heart and soul bereft
of the minutest mundane musing
will then sing and dance
for the King it has enthroned!

12. WHEN AND WHY?

Ever since the day I understood
the purpose of a human birth
I have tried to endeavor
to aim at attaining
but one destination, one goal,
one thought, one passion,
one innermost thirst...to know You Krishna
to realize You and love You
above anyone and anything
..... not to receive Your gifts
but to receive Your reciprocation
of my love!

For this loftiest of loves, I let go of
my worldly dreams and desires,
my pursuits for pleasure and prosperity
trying to obliterate 'me and mine'
to replace it with 'You and Yours.'

Weary of the ways and woes of the world
the heart could only turn to You
for solace, for shelter, for sympathy

and for a sure safe soulmate ......
the fountainhead of faith
the tallest tower of trust
the haven of hope!

All I asked for was to abide by Your Will
Why then was I misguided?
Why then did I cross ways with You within?
Why this irresolvable enigma again?
What do You gain here?
What would You want to teach?
The misery of losing material money
does not matter as much
as losing faith in my blatant beliefs.

Another unresolved question ......
another muddling mystery.....
another 'why' weighing on my wee self......
O when will wisdom whisper to me
giving me all my answers
with the realization of the Ultimate Truth!

13. LET ME TUNE IN TO YOUR WILL

You have flavored up
this wondrous world O Krishna
to give us a different taste every day.

It's sublimely sweet sometimes
and brutally bitter at other times....
while the teeth are still clenching
with a sly sour taste
the tongue begins to burn brazenly with hot spices.
Sometimes all is brilliantly bright
and sometimes dreadfully dark.

But amidst it all
You stand in Your *Tribhang Lalit* Form
peacefully playing tantalizing tunes
on Your flute .....
teaching me tactfully to accept
with unequivocal equanimity
the two sides of the coin.
You encourage me to wisely witness
happiness and unhappiness;
success and failure;

heat and cold
as nothing but different moods
of Your Cosmic Drama!

The moment I realize this
I begin to rejoice in
becoming a pawn in Your Hands
playing perfectly for Your pleasure.
Sweet serenity then snuggles in
when the self will begins to
smash into smithereens
as it tacitly turns
to tune in to Your Taintless Rhythm!

14. REMEMBERING YOU

Dawn dwindled into dusk.
Days dwindled into months
and months coalesced into years.
I have been waiting and waiting for You
but yet You did not come.

I downloaded and ogled at
so many beautiful pictures of You
and keenly searched for You
in innumerable temples and celebrated shrines….
but yet could not catch even a glimpse
of You, the Absolute You!

I heard so many songs, *bhajans* and *kirtans*
and screamed my lungs out glorifying You
but yet could not hear
the divine sound of Your flute.

I heard so many laudable *lilas* of You
from so many renowned saints and seers
but yet did not hear Your wondrous voice
that I have been fervently pining for.

I read innumerable books and all sorts of literature
that speak volumes of Your wonders
but yet I could not really understand
the enigma that You sometimes are!

But now I am desperate to delight in You....
to feel Your breath,
to experience Your touch,
to behold Your beauty and
to get mesmerized by Your flute call.
I yearn to perceive Your presence
and to comprehend the *'Tatwa'*
of Your Being O Krishna.
My inner being is desperately dying of thirst.
Please quench its parched heart
with the soul stirring shower of Your love!

15. WHAT NEED I FEAR

O Krishna
You are in my heart ....
Oh so close...
closer than my breath!
The calming caress
of Your care and concern
touches every moment of my life!
Your invincible arms
are a *kawach*
assuring me of eternal protection.
What need I fear then
any human or demon?

Your umbrella of mercy
is always open to give me shelter.
What need I fear then,
a rainy day?

You fulfil my minutest desire
and every single need.
Why do I need then
to hoard material possessions

or think of monetary security?
I am a billionaire of the rarest kinds
at the beck and call
of the Supreme King of kings
When I am completely His
Why wouldn't He be
completely mine!

16. PLAYER OF PLAYERS

O Krishna
You are the Ultimate
Player of players.....no doubt.
You are at the root of all thoughts....
right from the fleeting feeling
to the frenzy that froths up.

You are at the root of all actions....
You make me dance to Your twisting tunes
and then make me feel like a moron
crazily quizzing away....
Did I do right or did I do wrong?

Oh when will my mind
flow with the current
of the river of Your mind
or otherwise please give me
answers to all the questions
that block and blur my understanding
of You and all Your unique ways!

❀❀❀✱❀❀❀

17. A PERSISTENT LONGING

At times a desperate desire
to be with You alone ....my Krishna
oblivious to all existence
grips me so intensely
and emphatically ......
that my heart hankers
to soar up to Your skies.

But oh for my mad mind .....
how do I make it manage
to disentangle itself
from the dark, disturbing
dust and din
of disheartening thoughts....
futile and fruitless of a fragile world.

Unless I sweep out this dirt
from every nook and corner
of my murky mind
how can I invite You in.

I yearn and ache
for those marvellous moments....
when this mind magically merges
into Vrindavan
and every thought becomes a Gopi
dancing elegantly to Your tunes
for the exclusive Raas Lila!

18. SHAME ON ME

I have realized today
thanks to
Krishna's causeless mercy
that somewhere deep down
I believed that I was a good soul
and a good devotee
and have no *raag* and *dwesh*
but no .....I was unaware
of my deeply hidden *anarthas*
for which I must have taken
so many births.

If I was really as pure as I thought
why would I find faults in others?
How many times will He keep
showering His mercy on me
pointing out my faults
and giving me chances to improve?

While life still exists in this body
I must try to cleanse, polish
and sparkle myself.

if I had even an iota
of true love for Him
I would be quick to grasp
and digest His mercy.
I would be able to see Him in others
instead of finding faults in them.

O Nath, I cry from the deepest core
of my heart and from every pore
of my body
O please, please, please
give me the spiritual strength
to control my tongue
and my nit-picking mind
from finding fault in anyone
and for remembering forever
not to ever fabricate
any fault-finding word at all.

Allow me to see
the beauty of Your Being
hidden behind ferocious facades
O Nath I beg with full *dandwats*
to grant me this blessing and boon!

❁ ❁ ❁ ❁ ✺ ❁ ❁ ❁ ❁

19. PURE LOVE

Peerless and pure
let my love be for Thee...O Krishna!
Achieving this destination
of becoming taintless
will undoubtedly entail
tantalizing tests and trials.

I stumble and stagger
up the vain vertical path .....
breaking boundaries
of concocted concepts
as I strive to stride beyond
success and failure;
praise and blame;
honor and dishonor.

Oh when will I prevail over
the fear of fall and failure?
When will the ego of attachment
to all that I consider mine
dwindle to dust?

When will all my desires
dissolve into Yours?

Only then will I
truly understand You and understand that
true love overrides all thoughts,
beliefs and notions.
It is challenging and demanding
flowering from firm, unflinching faith.

Arjun in the Mahabharat
was asked to kill his kith and kin.....
his elders and teachers
whom he revered and respected;
loved and adored ....
But his deep, devout love
for You Krishna .....
made him accept Your Words
and follow Your Will.

When will I experience that
knowing You ....the One and Only
leaves nothing else to be known.
Serving You means
actually serving the entire universe.
Loving You is loving

all Your creation
and yet rising above attachment to all
to be conjoined to You alone.

When will I silently submerge
in the sweetest surrender to You
shaking off all the shackles of slavery
to the strong and shrewd senses!

20. I PAUSE TO PONDER

I pause to ponder
and I perceive Your powerful presence ....Krishna
as You passively peer and peek
at every deed I perform
at every word I voice
and at every teeny weeny thought
that transpires in
or transgresses my mind.

You promptly point out to me
with perfect precision.....
my follies and faults.
You guide and goad me
to be in harmony
with Your Will,
propitiously pulling me up
whenever I stumble ....
quickly stopping me
from falling.

You illuminate my path
with Your sparkling eyes

when I'm lost
in the darkness of delusion;
making clarity conquer confusion and
making carefulness convince carelessness
to take a back seat.
Your care, concern and constant companionship
overwhelm me and enthral me.

O Krishna
Knowing that You are
closer than the closest,
dearer than the dearest,
eternally by my side
and never abandoning me
even for a fraction of a second.....
I yearn to reciprocate Your love
that is peerless and selfless
but feel hopelessly helpless.

What can I give You?ll
No matter how big an offering I make
it will always remain
a tiny drop of a bottomless ocean!

So let me offer myself entirely .....
every inch of me…....

my mind, body, heart and soul
completely at Your service ……
at Your beck and call
every single second.

O my Krishna
the least I can do in gratitude,
is to not forget You
even for a zeptosecond!

21. OPEN-EYED SLUMBER

I realize and repent today
at this stage of life.....
how I have wasted so much
of my valuable time in
pursuing and practicing *prajalpa*....
worrying about worldly woes,
gross gossip that got me nowhere,
peeping into petty and paltry
pastimes of people,
voicing worthless words,
taxing and tiring my mind
with futile, fruitless and feckless thoughts,
engaging in aimless and expendable acts.

Every second that silently slipped by ...
without You as its axis
was a worthless wail ....
a moment of death in life!!
My heart is heavy
with remorse and repentance.

Even after understanding this
and experiencing the inexplicable taste
of Your Remembrance
my *sanskaars* silently spring up
to make the same mad mistakes
of indulging in unavailing actions
again and again.

Oh when will I wake up
from this open-eyed slumber?
O Krishna
I am absolutely incapable
of waking up from this hypnotic sleep.
All I can do
is turn to You with folded hands
let me free myself from the fetters
of these deep rooted *sanskaars*
that I am fenced in!

22. I AM INCAPABLE

Oh my beloved Krishna
You are showering mountains magnanimously
but meager as a molehill
is my capacity to receive
Your Grand Grace.

Your enormous eagerness to guide me
from moment to moment
flashes forth like lightning
but my slow snail like speed
fails to catch up with You.

My energy-less efforts to exist
constantly in Your consciousness
are all in vain.....
I ache and urge
for my mundane mind
to leave the material mud
of murky thoughts
and to travel to the
transcendental territory
where every atom of

pure consciousness is scintillating
with Your pristine presence.

No amount of the deepest mental speculation
can reveal You.
No ephemeral word,
thought or deed
can ever transcend to touch You
except for the purest and deepest
feelings and emotions of unconditional love.
O Nath
before my journey on this planet ends....
please ......freely fill to the fullest
my heart and my soul
with this rare, ravishing *rasa* of love
that You really relish!

23. INCREDIBLE CREATION

You are everywhere
within and without
say the seers
and yet
the ephemeral eyes cannot see You
but can only see everywhere
all that is not You
the mundane which is but *maya* —
Your external energy
that is forever deluding me.

Lost in this maze
I am at loggerheads
trying to understand
how to move
from *moha* to *nirmoha*
from attachment to detachment .....
from *asat* to *sat*...
from the unreal to the real .....
from the mundane to the metaphysical ...
from the earthly to the ethereal ....
and from the grossest to the subtlest .....

which seem to be
intricately interwoven
and yet are distinctly different.

I belong to the transcendental
am *sat chit ananda* like You
and yet I cannot possibly traverse
from the transient to the transcendental
because my material means
the mind, body, senses, intelligence and ego
do not have a valid passport
issued by You which alone
will allow me to travel to
Your transcendental territory.
I am pining for Your mercy to
break the *jada chetan granthi* within me.....
the knot where the *jada* ephemeral material body
meets the *chetan*.... pure consciousness.
and make me eligible to receive
this passport from You!

24. GOD CANNOT WALK FOR ME

He gave me legs
and the strength to walk
So walk I must.....
He cannot walk for me!

He gave me His Name
not different from Him
to hold me if I slip or stagger
and showed me an illumined path....
So walk I must.....
He cannot walk for me!

He gave Himself
as *archa vigraha*
to bestow His bountiful blessings
and boost me up
with His blissful beauty.
His sweet smiles
always encouraging me
in all my attempts
and endeavors to inch ahead .

So walk I must......
He cannot walk for me!

Oh let me walk and walk
one pointedly towards Him
without looking right or left.....
day in and day out.....
till my bones break
and I can walk no more.
Won't He then be moved to tears
and compelled to come down
to pick me up
and carry me back
to His heavenly home
as He did for
Shri Gajendra the elephant
whose potent prayers
persistently persuaded Him
to come down personally!

25. RADHA

O Shri Radha
poised on the peaks of
pristine purity and perfection....
Your Name contains
an endless ocean of love!

Love full of light and luster;
luscious and lively;
Love that is always
fresh, fragrant and flawless ;
unconditional and incomparable.

Love that never demands but fulfills
all that Krishna demands.
Love that never asks for anything
but gives everything.
Love that has no expectations, aspirations,
examinations, queries or questions.

You are nothing but
an embodiment of love
who alone can always be

with and within Krishna
whose every atom...is just
LOVE and love and love!

I humbly hold on to
Your Holy Feet.
O when will You
make me Your servant for eternity!

26. ON DEATH

Death....the inevitable
a sure fire reality ......a firm fact
accepted by all and applicable to one and all
and yet....
why the fear....the grief...the dread?

It will only destroy the dilapidated house called the body
and allow the ever living soul
to soar to new lands, new adventures and new discoveries
and yet....
why the fear...the grief....the dread?

Millions of desires fulfilled.
Life lived King Size.
No dearth of anything.
and yet.....
why the fear...the grief.....the dread?

Is it due to deep rooted attachments,
hidden desires awaiting fructification,
anxiety and apprehension of the inexplicable unknown?

Whatever it may be
but for me it is nothing but
a constant consternation
that my one and only aim of life
.....my absolute objective and
my ardent aspiration
of seeing, knowing and realizing
You.....Krishna
is assuredly and inevitably met with
and I am able to delve into
the depths of Your divinity
and not return to
janma, mrityu, jara, vyaadhi...i.e.
birth, death, old age and disease
before death surreptitiously sneaks in
to snatch me away!

I pine and pray to ponder
on thoughts of You then
that will be the meter to determine
if the life I have lived has been rightly lived.
As You say in the Gita:
*'anta-kāle cha mām eva smaran muktvā kalevaram
yah prayāti sa mad-bhāvam yāti nāstyatra sanśhayah'*
Meaning:
"And whoever at the end of his life,

quits his body remembering Me alone
at once attains My nature.
Of this there is no doubt."

27. DISPEL MY DISTRESSING DOUBTS

Oh for the feel of Your fingers
gently wiping my tears......
how passionately I pine!
Oh for the warm touch
of Your Hand on my shoulders
how lovingly I long.....
For the cool comfort of Your
compassionate glance
how crazily I crave.....
To dare to see You in a dream
dispelling my distressing doubts
how desperately I desire.....

But even though
You are closer than the closest
whispering as my constant conscience and
witnessing my tiniest thought,
word and deed ……yet
You leave me high and dry
and pretend as though I don't exist.
You love to remain
notoriously nonchalant,

callously cold and
absolutely indifferent!
Is this love *Deendayalu?*

O Krishna…..
my very existence cannot subsist/ endure
if You as my axis exit
as the sole support of my soul.
My faith in You
is the foundation on which I flourish
and if You fail me
I will flounder and fall
to be a failure forever .

O love of my life
light up these lonely lanes
I'm lingering on
to let my faith find
its flowers and fruits.
O *Karunasindhu*
uproot these weeds of doubt
and make my woes and worries
wholly wither away!

❀❀❀❀✱❀❀❀❀

28. THE ELIXIR OF LOVE

There is something invisible,
intangible, not easily attainable;
something that is indescribable,
exquisite, exceptional, extraordinaire
the topmost treasure.....
that alone is worth striving for
on this ephemeral earth
and in the transcendental territory beyond.......
and that something
is the elixir of love .....

Love that can bind the
Boundless *Bansidhar*.
Love that allowed *Maa Yashoda*
to bind her *Kanha* with ropes!
Love that brought
the king of kings Krishna
come down on His knees
to wash His friend Sudama's feet!
Love that made Parthasarathi
become Arjun's chariot driver!
Love that made

the most sought after Shyam
disguise Himself to seek Radha
begging and longing for love!

O Krishna
an insignificant *jiva* like me
undeserving and unqualified
begs for that exotic elixir .....
one drop of
whose extraordinary exuberance
can give an exhilarating
and exciting experience.
I cannot but crazily cry and crave
for more and more.
O Great giver of grace
please don't keep me
insatiated and unsatisfied.
I humbly beg again and again
to give me enough
to quench my thirst forever!

29. A HEAVY HEARTACHE

Every night
my heart heaves sad sighs
and the heartache gets heavier
as another dawn
dwindles into dusk....
another day filled with
moments and moments
goes by waving goodbye.....
smiling slyly
and questioning me,
"Have you seen Him yet?"
"Did your Lord respond
to your constant call and craving?"
"He is here before me," I say
"but my spiritual sight is blurred
with the dust and din of the world."
Each day my hair is getting grayer,
my limbs are languishing,
my voice is weakening
but this heartache hidden
behind hollow happiness
is just growing and growing!

Oh what do I do?
Where do I go?
How do I move through
this mysterious mist
that's marring me
from making me mindful
of my Madhav?
O Mercy please give
my spiritual vision an eagle's eye
so I can visualize Him
before my last twilight
on this earth!

30. LEAVE ME TO LEAD MYSELF ON

My Beloved has been waiting
eagerly and impatiently since aeons.
Lost in the luring lovelies
of the lower laurels,
I feigned He is not familiar
and foolishly felt
He is not a friend.

With my head held high
and my heart unheeding Him,
I wasted in this wild world
lifetime after lifetime ....
all my precious and priceless moments
in the dreary darkness of delusion.

I know now how
lovingly He lures me......
how benevolently He beckons me
and how this attraction to Him
allures and enthrals.
So I bawl and beseech with all my heart
only for my *Kanha* now.

I cock up my ears to hear
the faintest melody of His flute .
I vainly wait for a whiff
of His wonderful voice......
and for an invitation
from His angelic eyes.

O voices of the world
I plead and pray
with folded hands.....
please don't disturb me
from driving to
my desired destination.
All my duties to the dwellers here
are dedicatedly done.
Let my devotion to my dearest
not dwindle with distractions anymore.
Please leave me to lead myself on
to my love......to My Krishna

31. MY ONE AND ONLY

Even if I became a tiny speck of dust
at Your celestial Lotus Feet
locked up in Their warm embrace....
I would become oblivious
of my existence on this earth -
dukhalayam ashashvatam
as You have called it in the Gita....
alerting us since aeons.

Oh why did I ever desire to come to this planet
and why did I never desire
to go back to You....
a personification of pure love,
a haven of happiness
an abode of everlasting ecstasy.

Now as much as I would yearn to
I cannot take a big leap or fly up
to You......
I must wait patiently and tirelessly
for Your heart which has now become hard
to throw open its doors....

Fragrant Flowers At The Feet Of My Flamboyant Flutist.

and for the stretch of Your arms
to pull me up.

Oh when will Your entrancing eyes
bestow their benevolent blessings
on mine that ache to see You ....Krishna
the One and Only that I pine for!

32. THE HEART IS YOUR HOLY HAVEN

I travelled miles and miles around
from shrine to shrine,
from the mountain to the sea,
from pillar to post
but didn't espy You anywhere.
I embarked on this voyage to You
with all my vanity....
hoisting the flag of ego
on my ship loaded with *karmic* cargo.
But the Supreme Shore seemed
to be nowhere in sight....absolutely
imperceptible and unreachable!

No matter how earnestly I yearn
or put in all my energies and endless efforts....
but the ephemeral body will not endure.
sluggishness puts the soul in slumber.....
the mind mercilessly meanders mindlessly.
the intelligence is still dominated by dogmas.

Yet You are very much there
in the midst of all this.....

closer than my zingy breath
closer than a tingly thought
closer than my clingy skin....
happily hiding in Your eternal haven
in my heart within!
The distance between us is so meager
and yet You appear to be
further than the furthest!

Like a scintillating sapphire
You are shining in my heart
but unless I throw off the flag of ego
unload the heavy baggage
from the ship of my mind
and allow the storm in the sea
to calm down with the wise wind
of pure unconditional love.....
will the serenity of selflessness
silently seep into my senses
and sponsor me to see You
making me realize and relish
my *rasik Raas Bihari*!.....
My very own.....Shri Krishna!

❀❀❀❀✱❀❀❀❀

33. YOU ARE EVERYWHERE

O Krishna
Where are You not?
You are there high above
in Your spiritual kingdom
and You are here below
on this planet earth too.
You are far, far away and yet
nearer than the nearest
both within and without!

Pause awhile O *jiva*
and feel Him in Your breath
heaving in and out.
Go into the deepest chamber
of your heart
and hear Him throbbing
loud and clear.
Taste Him in the tingle traveling
in your nerves as you nurture
His nectarean Name.
Listen to His footfall
in a breeze that blows in bliss.

Rejoice in the rapture of raindrops
and thrill in the thunder
that are His mercy.

He is singing in the sea waves
and dancing with the ducks.
He is smiling in every smile
and luxuriating in laughter.
He is hiding in every heart
and peeping out of the pure.

Indulge in His innocence
when you see a baby smile.
Feel His warmth in
the wisdom of the wise.
Perceive His peace in a prayer
and eagerly await His response
when You cry crazily for Him.
O humans why are we hankering
for Him high and low
He is here and now!

34. TIME

O Time……
racing away recklessly …..
I try very hard to catch up with you
but dexterously and deftly
you dodge me somehow …..
and then look back
with a mischievous smile.

Sometimes your loud laughter
rankles within me
reminding me repeatedly
to resolve resolutely and robustly …...
to race you anyhow.

O why don't you put
a speed breaker
on your speedy pulse
to lower your blood pressure?

Please wait for me, I plead.
I will only fill you
with lotuses of love

offered at the feet of Krishna.
Their fragrance will be filled
with His remembrance
and each pretty petal
will proudly profess His Name.

When you hear
the magical melody of His fabulous flute call
You too will become still and statuesque
just as He makes the mobile become immobile
and the immobile, mobile!

I know you cannot give up your dharma
of being constantly on the move
unless you are
transported to the transcendental.
So instead I beg you of a favor
if I cannot catch up with you....
you can at least catch
every moment of mine
and offer it to Him
for whom I hungrily hanker...
if you grant me this grace
I will be graciously grateful to you forever!

35. YOUR PROMISE

I tried in vain to soar up
to the spiritual skies
with *japa, tapa* and
other endless efforts
but realised that
the ladder that leads up to You
is held by You.

I need to
firmly feel and fixedly believe
obdurately and unwaveringly
that it is You alone
that can help me to climb up
and absolutely no one and nothing else can!

I also realise that I cannot hold the ladder
if my hands are heavy with
concrete concepts and set beliefs.

I have unflinching faith now that
even if my practices are not perfect,
even if my mind makes mistakes,

even if my words are not wise and
my acts are not accurate and exceptional ......
it doesn't matter.

All I ache for now
is for the loftiest love and longing
that alone will lure You.
O Krishna I believe
stolidly and staunchly
in the promise You give in the Gita:
'Sarva-dharman parityajya
Mam ekam saranam vraja
Aham tvam sarva papebhyo
Moksayisyami ma sucah'
Meaning:
"Abandon all varieties of religion
and simply surrender unto me alone.
I shall deliver you from all sinful reactions;
do not fear."

36. WHEN WILL MY HEART ASSUME RADHA'S GOLDEN GLOW OF LOVE

When my Krishna
is displeased with me
how am I still able to
find taste in food?

When my Krishna
is displeased with me
how am I still able to
sleep soundly?

When my Krishna
is displeased with me
why doesn't my heart
mellow down and melt?

Why don't tears trickle out
in torrents from my listless eyes?
I don't even know what to do
to please and plead Him.

Oh when will my heart glow
with the golden glitter of

Radha's heart.
When will my mind
become Radha's mind?

When will my *swarup* and *swabhav*
surrender solemnly and solely to Radha?
O Radha, Radha, Radha
Whose mind heart body and soul,
whose *swabhav* and *smriti*
are filled choc-a-bloc
with Krishna, Krishna and only Krishna.
Who can see, hear, smell, taste and feel
nothing and no one but Krishna.
Her 'I' has evaporated,
Her desires have dissolved.
Pleasing Krishna is her only pleasure .....
satisfying His senses is her only satisfaction.

She exists only to enlighten us of His existence,
O Radha
grant me and grace me
with the golden glow of your heart
and let this gloss and glitter of love
draw Krishna's attention to me!

37. WHY DO I HURT YOU AGAIN AND AGAIN

How sloppy and shameless I am....
how utterly ungrateful and
how awfully arrogant.
Why do I hurt you again and again?
O when will I change Krishna?????

Time and again,
day in and day out,
year after year
You repeatedly remind me
not to find faults in others
and yet I am always so
captious, critical and cantankerous
......carping and cavilling.
Why do I hurt you again and again?
O when will I change Krishna?????

Don't the wise say that
we see faults in others
only when they exist in ourselves?
You are there within every being
hiding in the hideout of their hearts.

My earthly eyes are unable to X-ray
Your calm countenance
hidden behind the murky masks of man.
Why do I hurt You again and again?
O when will I change Krishna?????

I laugh listlessly at the loud labels
but fail to find
the flawless in the facade.
O Krishna
let the mirror of my heart
become so pure, peerless and paradisiacal
that it is able to reflect
Your ravishing radiance
wherever my earthly eyes fail!

38. PRACTISING THE PRESENCE OF GOD

I have been seeking Him
hither and thither
searching in holy scriptures,
temples and shrines.

Maybe I will find Him
if I shut myself out from the world,
maybe in the Himalayas,
maybe in the jungle,
maybe in severe austerity and penance,
maybe in deep meditation.

But the hidden Truth is that
God is here and now……
with each one of us
at every moment.

Let me try to feel
His powerful presence
in every breath.
Let me try to hear
His wonderful voice

in each throb of my heart.
Let me feel His luminous love
enlightening all the dark doldrums
of my mind.
Let me feel His existence
in the vibration of His Name
no different from Him.

There is nothing without Him .....
everything is His
every creature is His
and He is in everyone.
I too am His, to do His.

Let me be His perfect pawn
performing for His pleasure
remembering every moment
that I am here only
to serve Him with all sincerity .....
and to give Him pleasure in His play.

I pray to practise His presence
every moment....to please Him
my Only Precious Possession!

✿✿✿ ✵ ✿✿✿

39. WHO AM I?

I came into this world as a stranger
and began to identify myself as
belonging to the people and places around me…..
completely forgetting my original name, form,
relationship and the place I actually belong to.

I was lost in a mist of *maya*
and still am….
but since You have penetrated this mist
a bountiful beacon of blue beckoning me
to arise, awake and understand
my actual identity
which is ever eternal, all knowledgeable,
blessed with bliss and
always conscious of You, KRISHNA
a deep yearning to leave this labyrinth,
untangle myself from all attachments
and go back to where I belong is now building up.

But where do I turn?
How do I go?

Who will direct this disillusioned soul
To its divine destination?

O KRISHNA
when You are the divine Doer
and I am only a wary witness,
all I can do is …...
longingly look up to You with love
and lose myself completely in Your Consciousness
until I awaken again to find myself transported
to Your luring land of love!

40. A PLEA TO PATIT PAAVAN KRISHNA

I want to be a perfect person .....
pious, peerless and pure
to present myself properly
to You Krishna
but the insurmountable imperfections
that have usurped my mind
live like proud owners
who will not leave their premises
and I am too mild and mellow.
I lack the ability to be stern and strong
and to deal with them with a sturdy stick.

I vainly weep then, unable
to keep up
with my unrelenting resolutions
and wonderful vows.
A forlorn frustrated failure
I still face You
without the faintest fear.

The same story replays
day after day

year after year
and must have replayed
like a broken record
lifetime after lifetime.

I have nothing in me
no qualifications and no qualities
that can attract Your attention.....
but yet I have a feeble hope
and so plead and pray to You
if *Patit Paavan* is Your Name
You have to be true to it
to uplift a *patit* like me
and accept me
with all my faults, frailties and failures!

41. PAIN COMES AS MERCY TO DEVOTEES

My heart was afflicted
with agony and anxiety.
It was weak and weary
with woes and worry.

But the moment I sat for *kirtan*,
my fussy mind was forced
to focus on You
filling it with a fervent fever.....
a longing to leave the labyrinth
of life and just lay my head
at Your lovely lotus feet….Krishna.

A sudden realization then dawned upon me
that the happiness and unhappiness,
joy and sorrow, success and failure
that came and went
were like sun and shadow,
night and day,
laughter and tears,
that kept chasing each other....
but didn't matter

if I learnt to distance and disentangle myself
from its disastrous effects.

I sat within silently and solemnly,
waiting and witnessing the stormy sea
from the sanctity of the safe seashore.
I then rightly remembered
that Your warm and comforting Hand
was tightly holding mine…..
in this brutal battlefield
where I have no army and no arms
but for Your assuring Arm
that I am crazily clinging on to.

My heart then hollered loud and clear
to frighten agony and affliction.
I can understand now why
Maa Kunti prayed passionately
for pain and problems
which are not impediments
to the Omnipotent
but are actually stepping stones to Him
who alone is worth striving for!

Now I understand that
intense pain has immense power

to evoke the pure perception
of Your pristine presence
and that is why pain and problems
often visit Your true devotees
as nothing but Your Mercy!

42. NEGATIVITY TOO HAS A PLACE IN YOUR DIVINE DRAMA

I wondered why
winter followed summer;
rain followed sunshine;
and night followed day.
Why pain and pleasure;
success and failure;
perfection and imperfection
were so intensely interwoven.

But then I realized
that it was only
after experiencing intense pain
did I value the painless days of pleasure.
Success seemed sweeter
after feeling the frustration of failure
and the jab of jubilation
got enhanced after a sting of sorrow.

Deep is the density
of Your Divine Drama Krishna!
I frown at my flaws and faults,

my many mad mistakes and misunderstandings
but I also secretly smile to think
that were it not for them
would I have ever
relished and revered
the Grace that glows up my heart
and lifts up my spirit to soar up to the skies?

When I fail to perform to perfection
my devotional services,
it is my imperfections that make me
pine for perfection to please You.

Doubts and despair dampen the spirit
but the same drive me to dive
into depths of divinity too.

Moments of intense sadness
have actually been moments of
intense yearning for You.

Yes,   negativity cannot be negated…..
It plays a definite role
in Your divine design!

❁❁❁ ✺ ❁❁❁

43. YOUR HIDDEN HAND

O Krishna
As I look back at the path I have trodden.....
sometimes pitch dark
and sometimes dazzling bright;
sometimes paved
and sometimes muddy:
sometimes broad
and sometimes narrow;
sometimes high
and sometimes low,
I realize that the journey reveals
an uncanny underlying truth.....
that every nook and corner
and every bend and curve
had the lamp of Your Mercy
lighting up my path.

I fully understand now that
Your hidden Hand was always
warmly clasping mine with
loads of love, kindness and mercy
.....helping me to cross over

dreary deserts of disillusionment,

stormy seas of sorrow and

frightening fumes of the fire of fear.

O My Constant Companion

O Soul of my soul

O my *praan*.... my life.....

if all the stars of a clear night sky were words

I would still be in dearth

to express my thanks to You.

All I wish is to remember

in every breath of my existence

is that I belong to You....

and should live every moment only for Your pleasure!

44. O MY MIND

O my mesmerized mind
when will you rise from
the murkiness and madness
of this mundane world
that has enmeshed you
and entangled you since aeons?

Like a fickle fly
you repeatedly keep resting
on rotten reminiscences and on the
poor, painful and paltry passions of people.
These thankless thoughts
will only drag you down
to dwell into the dark dungeons
of despair and desolation
far from the dazzling daylight of divine denizens.

O my mind....I fold my hands before you
and humbly beg and pray....
with devout determination
desire and decide on a destiny
that will drive you to

the dear most dwelling place of
peace, tranquillity and love.
With undaunted devotion just dwell
only on Hari Hari and Hari
Just speak of Him, hear of Him,
see Him, think of Him and worship Him!

The pleasure that you pursue outside
is as momentary as a bubble.
Only Hari can give you
the higher heavenly taste.
Color yourself in His consciousness
and experience everlastingly
the euphoria of Krishna!

45. PRAYERS

Kirtan captivates the crazy mind
Naam Prabhu opens and unleashes
a reservoir of *rasa*
hidden in the heart.

Its first drop trickles out and
the transcendental taste
triggers a thirst
an ever increasing ache
an endless aspiration
an ever growing greed
to relish all the irresistible
rasa of the reservoir.

The heart hankers for its home
but cannot traverse from
the transient to the transcendental
as the tentacles of the transient
tightly tie it up.

Oh time, please pause and ponder
on the nostalgia

of the nectarean names of Krishna.
Oh my breezy breath
drink deep and devour
the intoxicating elixir....
and fill yourself with
its fantastic flavor and fragrance.
O my body bear the burden
of discomfort for sitting long
in the same posture
and instead rejoice in the *rasa*
of Krishna.
O worldly woes and worries
take wings and vanish.....
the wine of Krishna's mercy
is now working on me.
O *Naam Prabhu*
I plead and persistently pray
to perceive the pristine presence
of *Parameshwar* in You!

46. JUXTAPOSITION

Vainly whimpering with woes
the world today appears to be
....a .dreadful, disdainful *dukhalayam*
as Krishna says in the Gita.

When sorrow's siren so soul stirringly
soars surreptitiously
leaving joy silently sulking
in some remote corners;
When sin shamelessly shows
its shameful silhouette
and pain poignantly pierces people;
my heart bleeds and wonders
where You are!

O *Prabhu*
the seers say:
You exist everywhere
and in everyone.....
and scriptures too are screaming thus
but it is so hard to believe that
as a silent spectator and

as an indifferent unaffected entity
You exist equally in each living creature
and even in the most merciless,
in the most ruthless
and in the most torturous tyrant.

I really wonder how
You can remain a witness to
the ugly, abominable
and execrable activities
of Your own *anshas*...the *jivatmas*
and yet......
when I behold Your blissful beauty
so dazzlingly divine
I just know that You are nothing but
Karunasaagar, Deendayal
and all the endless adjectives
that glorify You!

When Your virile vibrations
make my nerves throb and thrill
with endless ecstasy .....
when Your deathless Divinity
makes my heart dance devoutly
and when in sweet surrender
my soul sings in symphony.....
I just realize

with Your monumental mercy
that the mundane murkiness
is nothing but Your *Maya* ....
that which is not You
an illusion....a temporary drama
created to run the *karmic* cycle.

Once this perception changes
it mellows me down making me
unruffled and unperturbed
with all that is occurring in existence
and I clearly understand that
though I exist in this mundane *maya*
I actually belong to You
the Ever Blissful, the Ever Beautiful
the *Satchitananda* Supreme
Personality of Godhead.....
and the more my eyes
will get entranced with You
the more will I understand
the intricacies of
Your Cosmic Play
and the less will I visualize
the vileness of the woes of the world!

47. TRUE DHARMA

Ethical conflicts sometime
confuse my mind.....
whether to do my daily worldly duties
with dexterity
or to give priority
to my devotional duties to God.

Worldly duties though difficult to define
and demand dedication
are nonetheless indispensable.
But even if done devoutly
sometimes fail to please
and if discrimination
doesn't draw a line
it leaves me dull and dreary.
Time and age sometimes do not permit
delving deep into mundane duties
leaving me in the doldrums.

I feel doubly disheartened
when my duties to Krishna
are not done in depth

with deep seated devotion
and dedication.
In trying to pursue to perfection
both duty and devotion
I find it difficult to discern and discipline myself
and wonder how to discriminate and do
what is most dear to Krishna.

Srimad Bhagwatam comes
to my rescue then and
drives me to a distinct and
definite decision.
It says:
'sa vai pumsam paro dharmo
yato bhaktir adhoksaje'
meaning:
the supreme occupation *(dharma)*
for all humanity is that by which
man can attain loving devotional
service *(bhakti)* unto
the transcendental Lord.

I realize that my primary duty
is to Krishna
and in order to dedicate
every moment to Him

I simply have to dovetail
every deed I do to Him
allowing myself to become
a perfect pawn He can use
as He so desires in His Cosmic Play.

I have to just remember and
put into practice what He says in the Gita:
'tasmat sarvesu kalesu
mam anusmara yudhya ca
mayy arpita-mano-buddhir
mam evaisyasy asamsayah!'
Meaning:
"Therefore , Arjuna, you should always think of Me in the form of Krsna and at the same time carry out your prescribed duty of fighting. With your activities dedicated to Me and your mind and intelligence fixed on Me, you will attain Me without doubt."

48. FAITH

My faith in You, O Hari
is like an immovable mountain
rock strong and sturdy .....
which isn't my creation
but one of Your innumerable gifts to me.

I did nothing to earn it....
neither irking austerities
nor pressurizing penances.
All I did was turn to You
and place my all in all at
Your divine feet.....
a sacred *'sukriti'!*

I trusted in You
knowing You are
my *Govardhan*
the magnificent mountain
that will withstand any storm,
wild wind or reckless rain.
I need no weapons to defend myself
when You are my *kawach*.....

the insurmountable shield
keeping me safe and secure
on the shore of this stormy sea of life.

When I am inadvertently anchored
to the feet of my Achyuta
I just know that
whatever happens in my life…..
whatever You will for me
will always be the very best.

Your love unconditional and incomparable
is what keeps me going
wanting me to keep alive
the flickering flame
even in the most tempestuous tornadoes!

49. THE SECRET KEY

O my Krishna
On the steep uphill climb to You
I come across so many pitfalls
so many deep desolate valleys
and so many
unknown twists and turns
but Your tender hearted grace
always brings me out
of the darkest dungeon.

I sometimes see
spots of glamour and glitter
that entice and allure
but again thanks to Your
benignant grace
I somehow realize that
they are misleading.

Seekers climbing up with me,
coming from different directions
firmly fixated in their own faith
try to impress upon my mind
their ardent beliefs but to no avail.

I come across bottomless wells
of knowledge that do kindle
a gnawing thirst in me.
I drink deep
but my thirst remains unquenched.

So tirelessly I trudge on
with a desperate desire
to seek You......
I do not possess
any magnificent merits
or exemplary qualifications.
I do not have any truckloads
of sincere *sadhana* to my credit
nor is my determination
made up of strong unbreakable mettle.

But Mercy's magical Wand
touches me again and again....
making me dare
to peep into Your *nikunj*.
Suddenly for a fraction of a second
Your benevolent eye
casts upon mine
and You throw me an invaluable Key
that opens the door to
a priceless treasure trove.

Realization like a radiant sunrise
lights up my long night to tell me
to turn my consciousness
from the wide world
and keep it constantly on You!

Even though weary of worldly ways
the world weighs heavily on me.
I robustly realize
that though I exist within the world
I have to not let it exist within me!

My mind ....like the moth
that meditates on the butterfly
to become like it
has to keep its consciousness
concentrated completely on You
by repeatedly remembering,
relishing and rejoicing in You!

An absolutely undeserving one
like me too can surely climb the peak
if it keeps its trust in You!

50. PAINFUL LOVE

Frivolous feelings silently swing
from one material mode to another
Satvik (goodness) *Rajsik* (passion)
tamsik (ignorance).

The emotion of love
is most enigmatic.....
sometimes heaping the heart
with heavenly happiness and
sometimes piercing it with pain
acute, agonizing.

When faith fizzles out
like the fizz of a fizzy drink
leaving it tasteless and insipid,
all I can perceive
at the zero hour
are dead ends and lonely lanes.

Wondering where to walk
I wander aimlessly.....
and look back at the doors

that coldly closed behind me
and wonder
if new ones will open
to explain the eternal enigma
of my relationship with You Krishna
An ageless affinity.....
an unbreakable bond
the closest confidante connection
the timeless truth
and yet
unseen and unknown!

Knowledge flashes for a while
like a firefly that flies away
in a fleeting moment
leaving me engulfed in
desolate darkness again.

Oh when will the Supreme Sun
Krishna rise up
to shine in my heart
and throw Light on
the puzzling secrets of the Soul!

❀❀❀ ✽ ❀❀❀

51. LIKE A RIVER TO THE SEA, LET ME JUST FLOW TO YOU

Like a perennial river
always full, flowing and frothy
You have lavished my life
with an abundance of everything!
There is no dearth of anything
nor a desire to dwell on
except for a constant craving
to just give myself in timeless totality
only to You, my Krishna!

Every word I voice
every thought I think
and every deed I do....
is only for You my Krishna!
Shri Krishna samarpan astu
Shri Krishna samarpan astu
Shri Krishna samarpan astu.

Even if I forget to express this
even if I forget to remember You
even if I am maddened

with mundane muddles……
no matter what……
but the core of my heart
the core of my existence
and the core of my deepest desire
is inadvertently anchored
only to You, my Krishna!

Like a river that can only give
all it contains and carries as it flows
to the infinite ocean
so also I give my all
in the sweetest surrender ….
only to You, my Krishna !

I know You will surely understand
my silent cries and
my wordless voice
for You are there within me
in the core of my heart
understanding me and knowing me
more than I understand myself
O my dear Krishna!

52. SEARCHING THE UNSEARCHABLE

You sometimes bless me
with an inexplicable experience
of exhilaration.....so abstract .....
much beyond the fathomless fantasies,
beyond physical phenomena
so intangible, inconceivable and unreachable ....
and yet I feel it with
the breath and the throb within me
giving me an inkling of Your
imperceivable Presence.

O Krishna, though You
are so much there within me
yet You remain eternally hidden
in Your holy hideout!
How I long to reach You
to see You, hear You and touch You!

I try to make my way up
on the ladder of *japa*
and though You inevitability exist
in every Name I repeat

but yet I wonder if it can take me to
the innermost chamber of Your Heart.

I try to pile up pious performances
which are impossible to perform
without Your invariable inspiration
but they too become powerless
to penetrate the impenetrable path.

I dive into the deepest ocean
of scriptural knowledge
and drown myself in it
and though You exist in every
wise word I visualize
yet I cannot catch even a
gauzy glimpse of You!

You have the uncanny knack
of existing everywhere
and yet nowhere
in the eyes of the avid
and ardent admirer!

Lost and limp, I now give up
the endless efforts to attain You
because now I understand that

it's all Your purposeful play
wherein You silently sneak into
the role of a seeker
and simultaneously be
the Sweet Supreme that
the seeker soulfully seeks!

53. THE TIME IS NOW

When the mellows and magic of Madhav
are so entrancing, enthralling and mesmerizing
then why does my murky mind
like a frivolous fly fervently flirt
with the filthy fantasies of all that is fake.

It pains me when I ponder
that You my Lord
are eagerly awaiting with open Arms
the arrival of this *jada jiva* .....and want it
to turn from darkness to light
from the ephemeral to the ethereal
from the transient to the transcendental ......
but vaingloriously the mind still wanders in the world.

Time will tirelessly tick away.....
transcending all traps
traveling with lightning speed…..
even the heavens cannot hold it
then how do we!

Days with their dazzling daylight will dwindle…
as the bonny body may deteriorate and degenerate.
Nightmarish nights may knock at the door
with shadows sneaking in.
The present and the future
will swish by into the past
in the twinkling of an eye
and before we know it
the game will be up!

The time is now, now and now
not a moment later
let me not allow it to slip by
without it holding a sweet thought of You!

54. HOW?

O Krishna
When You are everywhere
in each one and in everything
so subtly shrouded
and so hard to hold
like the fragrance in a flower,
the fire in wood
and the rain in a cloud…..
Then how will I find You
by delving into deep meditation?

It is unthinkable and unfeasible
for my ephemeral and terrestrial
body, mind and senses to
traverse the transcendental
and align with the ethereal
to which You belong ….*tat param*
then how can I ever reach You?

If *maya* is mesmerizing me
being a cataract

shutting my spiritual sight....
isn't she Your potency
at Your beck and call
who will gladly step out
the moment You step in?

The wise say the *saral* (simple)
can see.....
But how will the simple
comprehend the Complex....
Who can be attained
only by one in a billion?

When You are *kripa sadya*
and not *saadhan sadhya?*
then how will my *japa* and *tapa*
ever touch You?

Answers to these questions slowly spring up
when a deadly desire to know them drives me.
My conscience silently whispers within me:
If I truly love Him and want Him above all,
will I not naturally remember Him all the time?
Will I not do all that pleases Him
without worrying about how and when

I will attain Him?
When I have given my hand to Him,
will He not hold it and take me across?

GLOSSARY

Stuti: praise

Satvik: mode of goodness

Rajsik: mode of passion

Tamasik: mode of ignorance

Ananya: exclusive, one pointed

Samarpan astu: surrender to

Tribhang Lalit : Krishna standing in His triple bending posture

Kripa sadhya: attainable by grace

Saadhan sadhya: attainable by spiritual practices

Sadhana: spiritual practices

Lilas: divine play or pastimes of Krishna

Tatwa: axiomatic truth, fundamental element

Shastras: scriptures

Dharma: religious principles

Bhakti: devotional service to God

Karmic: to do with material activities that incur reactions

Naam dhan: God's name as true wealth

Praan: life

Smaran: remembrance of the Lord

Manan: contemplation

Nikunj: beautiful bower in Krishna's leelas

Japa: repetition of the names of God

Tapa: penance

Swarup: a devotee's true eternal form

Swabhaav: a devotee's true eternal nature

Patit Paavan: one of Lord Krishna's names meaning one who delivers the fallen.

Tribhuvanpati: one of Lord Krishna's names meaning the Lord of the three lokas

Mukunda: one of Lord Krishna's names meaning the giver of liberation

Sarvaloka Maheshwaram: one of Lord Krishna's names meaning the Lord of all the worlds

Dwarkadheesh: one of Lord Krishna's names meaning the king of Dwarka

Chappanbhog: food offerings made to the Lord consisting of fifty-six items

Radhanath: one of Lord Krishna's names meaning Lord of Radha

Achyuta: one of Lord Krishna's names meaning one who has never fallen

Loka: plane or realm of existence

sukriti: piety, spiritual merit

anarthas: anything which is not the goal, anything that is undesirable for devotion

raag: attachment or liking

dwesh: aversion/ hatred

prajalpa: useless talk, impediment to Bhakti

kawach: protective metal clothing worn by soldiers

Tat Param: in relationship with the Supreme Lord

About The Author

The author, Mrs. Jyoti Atul Bhatt's (Jaysheela Devi Dasi), life is a saga of the ubiquitous Indian woman - balancing several chores in life, swinging from her responsibilities as a homemaker in a joint family to a working woman She served as a Professor of History in Wilson College, Mumbai. Simultaneously she also enjoyed the seva of being the Director of the Indological Research Institute, Gurudev Siddhapeeth, Ganeshpuri where under the guidance of her first Guru, Swami Chidvilasanda, she progressed on her spiritual journey the seeds of which were sown in her by her parents. After marriage it was her husband Atul whose deep spiritual inclination and rich experience that encouraged and inspired her. Her two daughters, Janitri and Rudrika, who also indulged in spiritual practices with great zeal and fervor played a role in helping her on this path of salvation. In her quest for the Truth, the blessings and teachings of many saints and seers have left a deep, indelible impression on her heart. It was the philosophy and the uplifting teachings of Srila Bhaktivedanta Swami Prabhupada that gave her a definite direction on the path of Krishna bhakti where she has finally found repose. She took initiation from Shri Radha Govinddas Goswami Maharaj of ISKCON who helped to deepen her attraction for Krishna. She is striving to fulfil her intense desire to one day reach her desired destination of direct communion with Krishna and thereafter continue to serve Him eternally with undaunted devotion and love. She has offered her humble services to Him in the form of her first book, ' 'How Krishna Came Into Their Lives', some articles in magazines and newspapers, such as ' Shades of Dharma' and ' Sweet Surrender' in the Speaking Tree of the Times of India.

Made in the USA
Middletown, DE
28 April 2022

64872646R00085

Grail Yoga

by Edward E. Thomas
and the Editors of 24 Magazine

GRAIL BOOKS
A Division of East Ridge Press
Hankins, N.Y. 12741 U.S.A.

Second Printing, January 1976

Yoga

A GRAIL BOOK

Second Edition

Grail Yoga. Copyright © 1975 by The Church of the Way. All rights in this book are reserved. No part of the book may be used or reproduced in any manner without written permission except in the case of brief quotations embodied in critical articles and reviews. For information address East Ridge Press, Hankins, N.Y. 12741 U.S.A.

Library of Congress catalog card number 75-15207
ISBN: 0-914896-28-8

Pictures

Page 7: Drawing from *Del Cenacolo de Leonardo da Vinci de Guisseppe Bossi*. Page 22: *The Resurrection of Christ*, Rembrandt, from the Museum Alte Pinakothek, Munich. Page 26: *The Entombment of Christ*, Rembrandt, from the Museum Alte Pinakothek, Munich. Page 37: *Companions at Emmaus*, Rembrandt, from the Louvre, Paris. Page 39: *Christ at Emmaus*, Rembrandt, Musee Jacquemart-Andre, Paris. Page 51: Photo by William S. Gillies. Page 58: Photo by J. Allen Cash. Page 67: Photograph of Sri Ramakrishna from the Vedanta Society of Southern California. Page 72: *The Rape of Europa*, Felix Vallotton, from the Kuntsmuseum, Bern. Page 81: *Daniel's Answer to the King*, Briton Riviere, R.A. Page 85: *Help! Help!*, drawing by William Blake, reproduced by permission of Adrian van Sinderen Estate. Pages 96-105: Drawings by William S. Gillies.

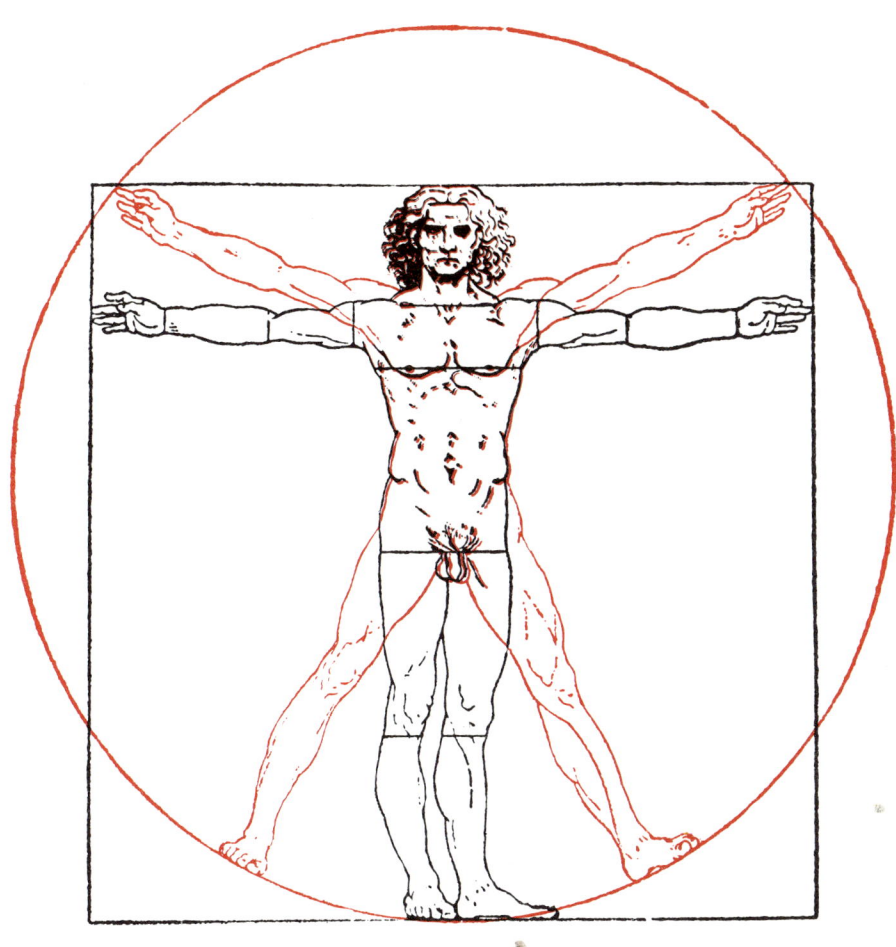

The human body—in its forces and in its very configuration—contains all the keys that are needed, with intelligence from higher levels, to unlock the riddles of human suffering, human freedom, and human regeneration. This fact is the basis of both Western and Eastern yoga. The drawing is a rendering from da Vinci's "Squaring of the Circle."

Publisher's Note

We are bookmakers who specialize in the literature of the Way. It needs saying that in the pursuit of the Way, books can be well used or abused. Reading is helpful and in most cases necessary, but it is no substitute for *doing the work* of the Way in obedience to the will of God.

Hear what a great master of the spiritual life (Caussade) says:

"The divine influence alone can sanctify us.... Without it reading only darkens the mind.... All reading not intended for us by God is dangerous. It is by doing the will of God and obeying his holy inspirations that we obtain grace, and this grace works in our hearts, through our reading or any other employment. Apart from God, reading is empty and vain and, being deprived for us of the life-giving power of the action of God, only succeeds in emptying the heart by the very fullness it gives to the mind.

"This divine will, working in the soul of a simple ignorant girl by means of sufferings and actions of a very ordinary nature, produces a state of supernatural life without the mind being filled with self-exalting ideas; whereas the proud man who studies spiritual books merely out of curiosity receives no more than the dead letter into his mind, and, the will of God having no connection with his reading, his heart becomes ever harder and more withered."

And further, by these, my son, be admonished: of making books there is no end; and much study is a weariness of the flesh.

Let us hear the conclusion of the whole matter: Fear God, and keep his commandments: for this is the whole duty of man.

Eccles. 12 : 12-13

CONTENTS

Foreword
PAGE 12

1
The Way of the Grail: The Yoga of Our Age
PAGE 15

2
What Arose? The Difficulties in Believing the Central Yogic Act of All Times
PAGE 21

3
Yoga Means Union:
An Interpretation in Eastern Terms
PAGE 45

4
Ramakrishna on Yoga
PAGE 63

5
Prerequisites of Yoga
PAGE 77

6
Surya Namaskars
PAGE 91

FOREWORD

A hundred years ago yoga was still esoteric, that is, for the few. Only an elite group really practiced it in the Middle East, the Far East, and the Christian West. And almost nobody in the world at large knew anything about it except as an outlandish and probably unsanitary eccentricity of the ever-charming but utterly impractical Orient.

Now, millions of people know about yoga, and some considerable numbers are trying to work with it. With the waning of religious and geographical prejudices, yoga has begun to appear as what it really is: the way of transforming human nature, the practical aspect of the Way, the Truth, and the Life.

It emerges indeed as the working know-how of the universal spiritual tradition, the Way, and not at all the private property of the East but a mine of knowledge and skill extending throughout the entire earth and strikingly present in the Christian tradition, and summed up in the Hidden Church of the Holy Grail. But the real powers of yoga—the powers that come after devoted and sustained practice—these are still very little known in both East and West.

You can read about these powers in the literature, but to find someone who has had practical experience of them and who knows at first hand something of both their blessings and their dangers—this is rare. The editors of this book know enough about them to have a very high regard for the blessings and a healthy respect for the dangers, to both of which we give due weight on the following pages.

Edward E. Thomas

Hankins, New York
June, 1975

1

The Way of the Grail

The Yoga of Our Age

THE WAY FOR MODERN MEN and women is the Way of the Grail. And the Way of the Grail is the axis on which the material and spiritual evolution of the human race turns. It is the yoga of the West, which includes the yogas of the East. It is the initiatic path of the present Age, which includes the initiatic wisdom and praxis of all ages.

The Way of the Grail is very high, very deep, and very special. But at the same time it is common, vulgar, in fact inescapable. It bears upon every man and woman. It bears upon you, whether you know it or not.

You may already be actively involved in the Way of the Grail and not know it. If you honor the truth, and serve it—if you love the good, and seek it—if you are trying, however humbly, to be a real human being—you are on this Way. Whether you can *stay* on the Way and *grow* on it and *succeed* on it depends on your courage and fidelity, that is, on your capacity for knighthood. Don't let the word put you off. It just means that you hang on to what you know is true and right, and live your life that way, without quitting or selling out. If you do that much, the Way will meet you, lead you, and support you.

The Way of the Grail is Christ-initiated, Christ-mediated, and Christ-centered, but it embraces all true ways. It never has been, is not now, and never can be a property of sectarians and bigots. The Way of Christ is inclusive and universal. It is the meeting place and melting pot of all the hopes, all the faiths, all the wisdom, all the energy and all the aspiration of all of mankind.

Recall for a moment *who Christ is,* and you will see that it must be so. He whom the Persians worshipped as Ahura Mazdao—he whom the Egyptians worshipped as Osiris and Pymander—he whom the Chinese worship as Teh and Tao—he whom the Hindus worship as Sat and Atman and Vishnu and Ishvara—he whom the Buddhists worship as Tathata and Tathagata and the Dharmakaya—he whom the Muslims worship as al Haqq and Allah—he whom the Hebrews worship as Aehyeh and Jehovah—*he* is the one true God. And *he* it is who has descended to mankind. There are not several of him; there is only one; there *can be* only one. And he now dwells in the earth in an essence which makes him both accessible and unavoidable. He has penetrated the planet to its core. He has infiltrated our land to its very rocks and trees, in a final campaign to rid it once and for all of its enemies.

The modern world is blinded by its immersion in materialistic illusions. But even as men grope in unprecedented psychic darkness, the real destiny of our race unfolds, and we all—comprehending or uncomprehending—play our parts. A great separation is taking place, and a great war is in progress—not one of our futile political or religious wars, with miserable egotistical ends in view, but a cosmic battle between Principalities and Powers—between the Sons of Light and the Sons of Darkness—with the fate of humanity and of every single human being hanging in the balance. In this struggle there are no bystanders. We are all combatants. The only questions are, do you realize what is happening? and whose side are you on?

It is in the midst of this intra-planetary convulsion that the Central Yoga of Humanity—the

Quest of the Grail—must now proceed. Heavily fated with the karma of past millenia, rooted in the primordial fault of the Adamic race, and rushing toward an aeonian climax and solution—these conditions are not a hindrance to the Quest; on the contrary, they constitute the necessary matrix in which alone the Great Work can be brought to its term.

The end of the Quest is the encounter with the *substantial reality* of God—spiritual *and* material—supernatural *and* natural—immense *and* immediate—divine *and* human. The goal of this Way is the meeting with Emmanuel, God with us—the Son of the living God in that radiant form which can be seen, touched, tasted, consumed, and assimilated—to our everlasting sustenance, health, and joy.

The trouble with it is, it seems too much. Nevertheless we are built for it and cannot live sanely without it. All attempts to defy it or escape it are doomed to endless frustration. The love of God is, finally, inexorable. As Jeremy Taylor said: He threatens terrible things if we will not be happy.

2

What Arose?

The Difficulties in Believing the Central Yogic Act of All Times

by Edward E. Thomas

PRACTICALLY EVERYBODY believes without a doubt that Franklin Roosevelt is dead. Yet the number of people who know *for sure* that he died (if indeed he did die) is very small. This small minority includes the medical people who examined the body and the undertakers who prepared it for the funeral.

The widespread acceptance of Mr. Roosevelt's death as a fact is based upon the testimony of a very few witnesses and belief in those witnesses on the part of the immediate circle of the late President's family and close associates. Everybody else's belief, mine included, stems from that small group of primary and secondary witnesses.

Now there is a possibility—however remote you may think it, nevertheless it *is* possible—that the whole country and the whole world have been deceived in this matter. It may be that Franklin Roosevelt was kidnapped—that a very cleverly-made wax effigy was presented as his corpse—that this effigy lay in state and was buried—that the doctors and undertakers were part of the plot—and that the family and the very close personal and governmental associates were either also part of the plot or fooled by the plotters.

I agree that this doesn't seem probable, but will you agree that it certainly is *possible?*

Roosevelt's death is taken for granted today solely and entirely as a matter of faith in the relatively very few witnesses involved. Fifty or a hundred or a thousand years from now some author who is hard up for a weirdo plot or who has some particular political or doctrinal viewpoint to peddle may raise the possibility that Roosevelt did not die at the time and in the manner reported. But such a book would hardly go now. We are too close to the witnesses, who, in spite of their small numbers, were reliable people, and some of whom are still alive.

(Note, please, that *history* has nothing to do with it. You cannot prove anything at all by history. History is merely a gathering and sorting out of what people have reported and believed to be true about events. History is a pot pourri of possibilities and probabilities. The value and utility of history are obvious, but it is among the least certain and least reliable of the academic disciplines. One should be very careful how one calls upon history to prove or disprove anything. If the present belief in Roosevelt's death remains unchallenged, that will go down as history; and if some day a great exposé occurs and it looks as if he was kidnapped after all, that also will go down as history; and way off in the future some big dome will hand down his mere guess as to which event really happened, and *that* will be the "history" of that time. Let the buyer beware.)

In the case of any event, the matter of witnesses is critical. If there are good witnesses, and particularly if there is a considerable number of good witnesses, the event will be accepted as a fact. And no matter how you question, investigate, interrogate, scientificate, or pontificate, you can not get above or behind or beyond the witnesses. They are prime evidence. And they really, actually, practically, and in fact do determine credibility.

The most widely circulated report of the past

several thousand years concerns a man who was killed—and then seen alive and physically active by over 500 witnesses during the six weeks immediately after his death.

In the centuries following, immense numbers of people all over the earth heard the story of this extraordinary event and came to believe, incredible as it is, that it actually happened.

Today, millions of people (many of them intelligent and reliable people) believe that Christ rose from the dead. But at the same time, millions of people (many of them intelligent and reliable people) believe that Christ did *not* rise from the dead. By appealing to numbers of people or quality of people who believe one thing or another about this matter, you can not prove anything. Or, you can prove it either way.

In the course of a long lifetime, I have been on both sides of this fence. When I was very young I believed that Christ rose, because I was taught it. Later on, I disbelieved it, because I honestly could not see how it could have happened, because I wanted to feel "emancipated" from the "thralldom of the past," and because it was the fashion of the times to disbelieve. Still later—when the realities of my own life had forced me to reconsider the weight of both early and late evidence—I came to believe that the resurrection was real after all. What I found finally *impossible* to believe was that the early witnesses—the 500-odd who actually saw the man alive after his death and the thousands who heard their witness—were either politically motivated frauds, myth-making muddle-heads, self-deceived religious or literary romantics, or

The sepulture of the dead Christ is described—by Anna Catherina Emmerick (1774-1824), a German peasant girl with ecstatic, stigmatic, and historical-clairvoyant gifts—as follows:

"The men now laid the sacred body on the leathern litter, placed over it a brown cover, and ran two poles along the sides. Nicodemus and Joseph carried the front ends on their shoulders; Abenadar and John, the others. Then followed the Blessed Virgin, her elder sister Mary Heli, Magdalen, and Mary Cleophas, the group of women that had been seated at some distance, Veronica, Johanna Chusa, Mary Marcus; Salome, the wife of Zebedee; Mary Salome, Salome of Jerusalem, Susanna, and Anna, a niece of St. Joseph. Cassius and his soldiers closed the procession. Two soldiers with twisted torches walked on ahead, for light was needed in the grotto of the sepulchre. The procession moved on for a distance of about seven minutes singing Psalms in a low, plaintive tone, through the valley to the garden of the tomb.

"The holy women sat down upon a seat opposite the entrance of the grotto. The four men carried the Lord's body down into it, set it down, strewed the stone couch with sweet spices, spread over it a linen cloth and deposited the sacred remains upon it. The cloth hung down over the couch. Then having with tears and embraces given expression to their love for Jesus, they left the cave. The Blessed Virgin now went in, and I saw her sitting on the head of the tomb, which was about two feet from the ground. When she left the cave, Magdalen hurried in with flowers and branches, which she had gathered in the garden and which she now scattered over the sacred body. Then she went back to where the women were sitting. The men raised the cloth that was hanging over the side of the tomb, folded it around the sacred body, and then threw the brown cover over the whole. Lastly, they closed the brown doors, probably of copper or bronze, which had a perpendicular bar on the outside crossed by a transverse one. It looked like a cross. The great stone, intended for securing the doors and which was still lying outside the cave, was in shape almost like a chest or tomb, and was large enough for a man to lie at full length upon it. It was very heavy. By means of the poles brought from the garden entrance, the men rolled it into place before the closed doors of the tomb."

otherwise merely credulous fools. It seems to me that there is no basis for any of these assumptions. But the only alternative is that what these witnesses reported to have happened *did* indeed happen, and that is my present position. I am not going to argue further in favor of this position, however, because I want to move beyond it to another point.

In order to go where this inquiry intends to go, I must ask one thing of the reader. I do not ask you to change your beliefs. I do ask you—regardless of what you have previously thought and for purposes of this discussion—however tentatively and with whatever reservations *to entertain the possibility* that the resurrection was an actual physical occurrence approximately as reported. In other words, keep an open mind. If you can not or will not do that much, you will not be interested in the rest of this chapter. Because I am going to raise questions which *follow* from the question, "Did he rise?"

I am going to ask, "If he arose, *how* did he arise? *What* arose? What walked out of the tomb? The resuscitated body of a man who had not really died? A ghost? A 'materialization'? The revived body of a man who had actually died and actually come to life again? Or was it *something else*? And if so, *what*?"

First, the question of resuscitation of a not-really-dead man. This view says that Christ did not really die on the cross but was rendered deeply unconscious, was taken down and entombed, and then later revived and smuggled out of the tomb.

In certain ways it is an attractive theory. At

one stroke, it gets rid of the whole problem—so incredible and indeed so *revolting* to the modern mind—of a human being surviving death under any circumstances. Modern man is not merely repelled but psychically nauseated by any suggestion that the supernatural may be real. The resuscitation theory enables us to allow some kind of event to have happened, while at the same time sparing us the really very unpleasant gulping and retching and gagging that most of us go through when supernatural implications seem unavoidable. And they *are* unavoidable if a man who had been really dead really walked out of the sepulcher.

The stolen-body explanation—which says that Christ really died on the cross and was entombed but that his followers later stole the body and spread the story that he had risen from the dead—has some of the attractive features of the resuscitation theory, chiefly in that it spares us the distress of confronting the supernatural.

Both of these theories were advanced almost immediately following the crucifixion. And since they are reasonable explanations, and since some pretty heavyweight authorities were active in their dissemination, they were widely believed from the beginning.

Both explanations, however, are loaded with difficulties. The resuscitation theory assumes that a group of Roman legionaries, who were assigned to execute a man whose death was a matter of prime importance, did not know their business and bungled the job. This is in the very highest degree improbable. The theory assumes that a man could live after receiving the

The first reported appearance of the risen Christ to a human being was not an appearance to the soldiers (who saw light and an angel but not the Christ), and not the well-known appearance to Mary Magdalene as given in John 20 and Mark 16, but an appearance to Joseph of Arimathea as given in the Gospel of Nicodemus. It is noteworthy that Joseph stands at the fountainhead of the Way of the Grail. The report of Christ's appearance to him is given in Joseph's own words, in response to later questioning by the elders, priests, and Levites who had imprisoned him:

"And Joseph said: On the preparation day about the tenth hour ye did shut me up, and I continued there the whole sabbath. And at midnight as I stood and prayed the house wherein ye shut me up was taken up by the four corners, and I saw as it were a flashing of light in mine eyes, and being filled with fear I fell to the earth. And one took me by the hand and removed me from the place whereon I had fallen; and moisture of water was shed on me from my head unto my feet, and an odour of ointment came about my nostrils. And he wiped my face and kissed me and said unto me: Fear not, Joseph: open thine eyes and see who it is that speaketh with thee. And I looked up and saw Jesus and I trembled, and supposed that it was a spirit: and I said the commandments: and he said them with me. And ye are not ignorant that a spirit, if it meet any man and hear the commandments, straightway fleeth. And when I perceived that he said them with me, I said unto him: Rabbi Elias? And he said unto me: I am not Elias. And I said unto him: Who art thou, Lord? And he said unto me: I am Jesus, whose body thou didst beg of Pilate, and didst clothe me in clean linen and cover my face with a napkin, and lay me in thy new cave and roll a great stone upon the door of the cave. And I said to him that spake with me: Show me the place where I laid thee. And he brought me and showed me the place where I laid him, and the linen cloth lay therein, and the napkin that was upon his face. And I knew that it was Jesus. And he took me by the hand and set me in the midst of mine house, the doors being shut, and laid me upon my bed and said unto me: Peace be unto thee. And he kissed me and said unto me: Until forty days be ended go not out of thine house: for behold I go unto my brethren into Galilee."

coup de grace—a lance thrust under the ribs and into the heart*—at the hands of a trained legionary under orders to ensure the condemned man's death. Nobody has ever suggested that the thrust was not given. And the speculations that it was ineffective seem feeble to the point of nonsense.

Finally, supposing that either the resuscitation or the stolen-body theory is true, in the first case one of the great spiritual teachers of humanity was a fraud, and in the second case one of the world's great religions is founded on lies spread by a group of frauds. Just think about that for a minute and see if you can believe it. I wonder if anybody really can?

But if it was not a matter of resuscitation or body-stealing, then we have passed beyond natural possibilities, and that brings us to supernatural or preternatural possibilities. To these possibilities the mind of modern man is strangely and, one is forced to say, pathologically hostile. To inquire why this should be so would take us on a side trip too extensive for this book. Enough to recognize that it is indeed so and that almost nobody escapes some degree of this very odd, very deep, and very illogical prejudice.

Can you stand a few definitions? They will help.

Nature is literally "that which is born." It is that which emerges from the latency. It is the phenomenal manifold. It consists of qualities

---

* See *A Doctor at Calvary*, by Pierre Barbet, M.D. (P.J. Kenedy & Sons, New York). Chapter Seven, "The Wound in the Heart," pp. 113-127.

and forms. Greek *physis* equals Latin *natura*. Physics is the study of nature. It is *the* natural science.

The *supernatural* is that realm of reality which is prior to nature in the order of essentiality. Nature comes from it and depends on it; it, on the contrary, does not depend on nature but radically transcends nature. Without the supernatural, there would be no nature. Without nature, the supernatural would continue to be exactly what it always is. The supernatural is the source, support, and end of everything in nature. Nature, on the other hand, can add nothing to the supernatural and take nothing away from it. The supernatural is the divine.

(Modern men generally have a simple but firm conviction about the supernatural. They believe either that it has no reality at all or that, if it is real, it is remote, irrelevant, and unimportant. This modern view is *sheer superstition,* based upon arbitrary and illogical inferences from the natural sciences and chiefly from nineteenth-century physics, and having no basis whatsoever in real investigation, unprejudiced experimentation, or anything remotely resembling true science; and certainly it has no warrants at all in really modern physics.)

The *preternatural* is an interesting and useful area to know something about. It is not the supernatural, and yet it is not "nature" as we commonly know it. The preternatural is that part of the phenomenal manifold (and it must be huge) which is beyond our ordinary knowledge of nature and ordinary inferences about nature.

A ghost is a good example of what we are talking about. A ghost is by no means a supernatural reality, but neither is it an ordinary natural phenomenon; it is, precisely, a preternatural reality.

One thing seems sure: The risen Christ is not a ghost. He says specifically that he is not, and he takes pains to prove that he is not. He tells the witnesses to touch him, saying, "Look at my hands and feet. It is I myself. Handle me and see. A ghost (*pneuma*) doesn't have flesh and bones as you see I have." And while they still hovered between fear and joy, to reassure them further he said, "Have you got anything to eat here?" And they gave him a piece of broiled fish and a honeycomb, and he ate it before them.

A ghost, by the way, is not an imagination or a hallucination, that is, a subjective phenomenon. A ghost is a "disembodied soul of a dead person believed to be an inhabitant of the unseen world or to appear to the living in bodily likeness" (Webster). It is an objective reality in the realm of the preternatural.

While we are on the subject, a word about hallucinations: It is quite impossible to "explain" the post-resurrection appearances by throwing them into this handy modern waste basket. To do so would mean that *all* of the people who saw the risen Christ were delirious, intoxicated, or psychotic, and obviously they were not. Remember that over 500 persons saw him at one time. If you want to try a little scientific experiment, just assemble 500 schizophrenics, or any assortment of 500 psychotics, drunks, or delirious people that you please, and see if you can get them all to hallucinate the same thing at the same time. Better not push the experiment too far, or you will end up having some bats in your own belfry.

But back to the preternatural. The only other possibility in this area is the psychic phenomenon which is known as a materialization. My own view of this question has been well expressed by Thomas E. Powers in *Death, and Then What?* Powers has actually seen a number of materializations, and so have I, and I agree with his evaluation of the phenomenon. He says:

> The notion, sometimes advanced by spiritists, that the resurrection body of Christ Jesus was a "full-form materialization" seems to me very far from the truth, little as we are able to comprehend what the full, staggering truth must be. Anyone who (as I have) has seen a variety of the apparitions materialized by the process of mediumship should be able to witness that these grotesque creatures must be almost as remote as anything could be from the embodied Reality who arose triumphant over death and appeared to men on that first Easter morning and afterward. A "full-form materialization" is invariably a kind of larval phenomenon, almost always confined to the dimmed-out or darkened séance room. If that is all the risen Christ signifies, then indeed, God help us! our faith is horribly in vain.

Well, then—if what rose from the tomb on the first Easter morning was not a materialization, not a ghost, and not a hallucination, what *was* it?

Was it the body of a man who was really dead and then actually came to life? The answer clearly is, yes. And that would be a sufficiently amazing event, if that were all of it. But there is more, and here is the real difficulty. The body

On the opposite page you see a painting by Rembrandt of the supper at Emmaus. On page 39 is another Rembrandt, also of the supper at Emmaus. The first painting is very well known, indeed famous. The second is very little known, and this is odd, because the two paintings belong together; one is a sequel to the other; together they show one of the most electrifying events in human experience.

You know the story of Emmaus. At the time of Christ it was a village about seven miles from Jerusalem. On the third day after the crucifixion, Cleopas and another disciple are walking from Jerusalem to Emmaus. The risen Christ approaches, joins them, and talks with them as they walk, but "their eyes were holden" so that they do not know him.

Christ asks them, "What is all this talk, and why are you so sad?" And Cleopas says, "Are you the only stranger in Jerusalem who hasn't heard about the things that have happened there these past few days?" And the still-unrecognized Christ asks, "What things?"

And they say, "About Jesus of Nazareth, a prophet mighty in deed and word before God and all the people. Our chief priests and rulers handed him over for execution and had him crucified. And we were hoping that he was the one who was to come and set Israel free . . .

"And some of the women of our company went to the tomb at dawn and found it empty, and they said that they had a vision of angels who said that he was alive. Some of our people went to the tomb and found things as the women had said, but him they did not see." Christ rebukes them as slow believers, and beginning with Moses he expounds to them the passages in all the scriptures referring to himself.

They draw near to the village, and he makes as if

he were going further, but they say, "It is getting late. Stay with us."

And he goes in and sits down at supper with them, and takes bread, and breaks it, and gives it to them. Now turn the page and see what happens next.

The very same scene as in the preceding painting is shown here—ten seconds later.

As he was breaking and giving the bread, their eyes were opened—and they knew him—and he vanished out of their sight. Rembrandt has masterfully recorded the tremendous instant—the chair overturned, the thunderstruck disciples, and the body of the Christ in the very act of dissolving in light. Here obviously is no allegory, no poetry, no myth. Here is a physical event, depending upon a degree of spiritual development and an intensity of living power radically transcending the ordinary, exceeding the range of our understanding, yet urgently demanding to be understood.

Rodney Collin (in The Theory of Eternal Life) *observes that it is not only miracle (the intrusion of a higher order into the lower) but miracle on a new level: "Nearly all the miracles attributed to Christ during his life refer to the healing or making normal of the physical body. . . . The miracles after the resurrection, however, are of a different order. Christ was then able to project a new physical body, or many such bodies, in different places. . . . Suddenly two friends, walking in the country to Emmaus, find a physical Christ beside them: the same day another Christ appears to disciples inside a locked room: a week later there is another appearance to Thomas under similar conditions; while a fourth Christ comes to disciples fishing, across the Lake of Tiberias. In each case, a very curious proof of physical existence is made by the appearing Christ himself, who insists*

upon eating food or being touched. This would seem curiously irrelevant, were its aim not to show that the appearance is no hallucination, even no vision, but an actual physical body. For those who understood, this alone would be proof that Christ had reached a realm where he could create and destroy bodies at will, that is, he had complete freedom of all vehicles, and was working in the spirit from the electronic world."

which rose from the dead is the same body which the man occupied before his death—*and yet not the same body*. It has the marks of the cruel treatment he received in the course of his trial and execution. It has flesh and bones like any other body. And it eats ordinary men's food. Thus far the sameness.

Now for the differences—and they are *very* strange: In this solid flesh-and-bones body the man appears suddenly in the midst of a group of people in a room to which the door is closed and locked. He disappears—simply vanishes—before the eyes of two men with whom he had been visiting. He is recognizable to many as the same man he was before his death—and at the same time he is *not* immediately recognizable to several of those who knew him best (Mary Magdalene, John, Peter).

What are we dealing with here? Obviously with a *radical mutation in human nature.* There have been indications throughout history of what was coming—in forerunners like Enoch, Melchizedek, Elijah, and al-Khadir. And now here at last we have the first fully developed specimen: *a new kind of man.*

And why not? There have been radical mutations in other forms of organic life. Why not in man?

We must try to understand our position as non-mutants in the presence of the mutant. We must not assume that we would have been any brighter about it than most of his contemporaries were; indeed, to this day we have not been very bright about it. But this is inevitable. *We cannot help* but regard the mutant with uneasiness, deep suspicion, and finally terror—from which the handiest recourse is disbelief: blind insistence that the mutant doesn't really exist, that he is an invention, a false rumor, a myth—anything, anything to get rid of him.

God knows, our terror of him is well founded. Because all of his shocking and liberating possibilities are built into each one of us, right down to the least of us. *We could be what he is.* There is no way to hide from this intuitive, instinctual, bone-deep knowledge. And we dread it, because we are desperately afraid of the change, and the cost.

What is he like, this new man?

First of all, he is what we all know a real man ought to be: He is *totally loving* in the exceedingly important negative sense of non-violent, non-retaliatory, and non-harmful to his fellow men, and in the positive sense of spending his whole energies in helping, healing, supplying, teaching, encouraging, and inspiring others.

He is *totally faithful to the truth,* regardless of consequences and regardless of what is tactful, prudent, politic, convenient, or expedient in ordinary human terms; that is, he doesn't lie for any of the usual reasons, or for any reasons. He is a man without a price; you can't buy him by any kind of favor or any kind of threat.

He is *totally concerned with God,* totally submissive to God, and so totally free in God. He knows the two things that a man, a real man, must know: He knows God. And he knows himself as the child (not merely the creature) of God and therefore in substantial identity with God.

He never confuses this self-realization with the merely personal aspect of himself, and thus he is *totally sane*.

He has *extraordinary vitality,* which he expresses most often in preternatural healing of all kinds of mental and physical diseases; and he has *extraordinary command of nature:* he walks on water; he changes one substance into another; he speaks to a storm and it immediately subsides.

Finally, *he dies in a radically new way* with radically new results. In the death of ordinary men, the spirit completely loses control over the physical body, which becomes inert and decays. The new man's spirit not only regains control of the physical body after death but does so with such an enormous access of vital and spiritual power that the body is transformed in appearance, in substance, and in function—literally raised to a new level of being.

Why should we say that this is impossible? Why shouldn't we meet this demonstration and challenge in the spirit of our age—the spirit of scientific experiment?

The new man has given clear instructions to be followed by anyone who wishes to prove to himself whether such power, such freedom, and such beauty are possible for men.

Doesn't it seem foolish to merely argue the case, when we might be following the instructions?

3

Yoga Means Union

An Interpretation in Eastern Terms

by John Burns

IF ANYBODY IS GOING TO TALK to you about yoga, you ought to know what he himself has done about it. So I will begin by telling you something about myself.

In 1939 my wife was in the hospital after having had our first baby, and I was trying to keep house in our home in Stanford, Conn., when a friend from Detroit came to visit.

George, this friend, was a person who was interested in a lot of things, a very alive guy. (Unlike myself. At that time I was interested in business, my family, golf, and getting drunk now and then. Period.)

George had a book with him which he either loaned or gave me, I am not sure which. I hope it was gave, because I still have the book, and I would hate to give it back, because it is a very useful book and surely out of print by now. Of course I would give it back if George insisted. If George reads this, will he please straighten me out?

Anyhow, I got this book. It was called *Yoga Explained* by F. Yeats-Brown, the man who wrote *The Lives of a Bengal Lancer*.

I don't remember what I had thought about yoga before that, probably nothing. Like everybody else, I couldn't be bothered with any weird stuff or foreign ideas or stunts. So yoga, if I ever heard about it, didn't make any more impression than, say, Eldorado or the abominable snowman—stuff I might look into some day but probably not.

But George said this yoga was solid in a certain way. He had tried it, and some good things had happened. So I read the book rather carefully, and *I* tried it. That is, I sat on the floor every morning with crossed legs and kept still for a while. And after some days it did begin to produce a remarkable state of quietness in the mind and body.

I must have done it daily for a couple of weeks, and I had enough sense to see that indeed there might be some very important possibilities here for anyone who would get into it and really work at it.

But in those days I was getting my peace and my highs from a much more convenient source —alcohol. And so the whole yoga thing got lost and the book ended up on a back shelf.

Very eventful years followed.

What happened, briefly, is that the sharp business man turned into a crazy man. I actually went psychotic. It was a very great surprise to me. Very shocking to my ideas about myself.

I was in mental institutions twice for psychosis and in hospitals seven more times for alcoholism. From a self-confident and self-satisfied man I became a fearful and desperate man, a stroke of good fortune which I did not much appreciate but which nevertheless woke me up enough to get interested in God and in a new way of life.

And that is how the yoga book came off the back shelf and into use once more. I did not begin to experiment with this ancient discipline again until I was several years into the new life and into its primary disciplines of honesty, turning to God, confession and restitution, prayer and meditation, and helping others.

Somewhere along the line I saw two things: I

saw that I had better re-connect with the religion I was born into. And about that same time I also saw that yoga was a *way* to do what I now wanted to do. I saw that it was a distillation of centuries of very practical know-how in doing precisely the things which my new way of life specified.

Around 1948 and 1949 I really began to study and practice yoga in earnest, so I have had over twenty-five years of sustained work at it. I am presently a business man, a family man, a member of Alcoholics Anonymous (John Burns is a pseudonym), a member of the Anglican Church, and along with it all a yogi. The term is nothing to balk at. Yogi (or yogin) merely means one who seriously and regularly practices yoga, and I do.

Different people have very different capabilities with regard to yoga. My own, for many years, were quite limited; but recently, the last five or six years, they are less so.

And that is enough personal identification.

Now, then—what *is* yoga?

I do not want to get into a big thing on definitions, but we need to be clear about what we are dealing with. Very simply, yoga is the *practical* part of the Way. Yoga includes theory of course, but the word really indicates practice. Yoga is what you *do,* how you *go,* in the Way. If you practice your religion, that is yoga. If you practice the AA program, that is yoga. If you practice any kind of sane ethical principles, that is yoga.

Yoga is a universal thing, by no means confined to the East. Moses, Jesus, and Pythagoras were among the great yogis of all time, and they

There is a lot more to it than this. Yoga is sometimes mistakenly thought of as consisting mainly of postures and exercises. Posture is an important part of it, but only a part. If you are physically disabled and can do no postures, you can still do yoga and do it beautifully.

Yoga is a whole way of life—the way of living in order to travel the Way. Posture is the part of yoga that trains the body and vital force and stabilizes them as a base for prayer and meditation. And these latter in turn are not ends in themselves but means to the end of knowledge of one's own higher levels and finally of God.

Posture (asana) is one of the eight "limbs" of raja yoga. The asana shown here is the full lotus (padmasana), with the throat lock (jalandhara bandha), and with the hands in the unextended gesture of knowledge (jnana mudra). The yogi is an elderly (pushing 60), Western, square Christian with a long history of serious illness, from which he has recovered as a result of participation in the Way.

were *gurus* of succeeding generations of yogis.

Over the centuries yoga has been practiced not only on the banks of the Brahmaputra and the Ganges but also on the banks of the Hwang Ho, the Oxus, the Tigris, the Jordan, the Nile, the Volga, the Rhine, the Seine, the Thames, and the Mississippi.

All religions are forms of yoga. And so are a lot of other activities. Work, done with intelligence and unselfish devotion, is yoga. The right expression and control of sex is yoga. Study in the search for truth is yoga. Masonry is a form of yoga. So is the ballet.

But there are well proved and well marked main lines, consisting of four major kinds of yoga. They overlap, and one kind of yoga, if practiced well, eventually develops to include the other three kinds.

There is (1) the yoga of love and devotion (*bhakti yoga*)—(2) the yoga of intelligence and knowledge (*jnana yoga*)—(3) the yoga of work and service (*karma yoga*)—(4) the yoga of training, exercise, and discipline (*raja yoga*).

All great yogis include all forms of yoga in their lives, but each is apt to demonstrate one form more prominently than the others.

In India in the past century there have lived four great exemplars of the major yogas. Sri Ramakrishna was a great bhakti yogin. Sri Ramana was a great jnana yogin. Mahatma Gandhi was a great karma yogin. And Sri Aurobindo was a great raja yogin.

You will think of many more, throughout the centuries and throughout the world: St. Anthony the Great is a terrific raja yogin; (indeed, he is the prototype of raja yoga in the recent West). Jalal al-Din Rumi is a tremendous bhakta. Isaac of Syria is a towering jnani. Martin Luther King is a great recent karma yogin. Searching history, you will find many others whose characteristic yoga is obvious.

Anyone anywhere who wants to know God and is doing something about it is a yogi.

But "know" is a very strange word, and one of the first steps in yoga is to learn to use words carefully.

When the Sepher of Moses says that "Adam knew his wife, and she conceived," it is not using "knew" as a euphemism. It is making the point that *to know* in any real sense is to *unite with*.

And precisely *that* is what yoga is all about. That is what the word means: union.* Yoga is the art and science of union, not only of man and woman, but of the human being and God.

To reach the goal of yoga is to know God by a transforming union.

Now maybe you will think that that is somewhat extreme as to altitude. But if a man will not aim that high, eventually he will get sick and deteriorate. Man is made to know God. If he tries to stay on middle ground too long, he does not thereby enhance his humanity; he falls below the human level into the bestial—or comes apart from the human into the diabolical.

It is a mistake to start so important a thing as yoga without first having some intelligent idea of what you are getting into. And the realities involved are such as to powerfully stretch the

---

* *Yoga* comes from the primitive root *yug.* Our own words *yoke, join,* and *unite* come from the same root.

mind of anybody who tackles the subject.

So here we go.

The first point to be made is a puzzler. Yoga is the science of union, but it seems that *there is nothing to be united.*

God in the universe (Brahman) and God in man (Atman) do not need to be joined. They are eternally a unity. Atman and Brahman are one. I and the Father are one.

Then what needs to be joined?

Not jiva (the individual, personal self) and Atman (the indwelling divine Self). There are not two selves but one. All selves everywhere are only nominally and formally separate. *Essentially* they are one with each other (I am to love my neighbor *as* myself because he *is* myself). And essentially all selves are one with God (what I do to the least of my brothers I do to my Lord).

Well, then, what is the problem? If I am already in union with God and with my fellow man, what is all the excitement about? Why all the talk about yoga and union? Why should I spend a lot of time and work to get something I already have?

Note the following: the unity of myself and all creatures in God is an eternal reality. But *in me and my kind* it is smothered and very effectively obscured by what is called the ignorance (*avidya*).

Not ignorance, mind you, but *the* ignorance.

The ignorance is not mere absence of knowledge. The ignorance is a positive power which has the capacity of *veiling*. It veils my own Self, veils God, and veils higher or essential objectivity.

This veiling is not a complete hiding but an obscuring. We experience reality but in a diminished and distorted way, and therefore we continually misunderstand it and underestimate it.

The ignorance produces a condition of hypnotic trance—precisely a light hypnotic sleep in which the subject feels himself to be awake, is able to function, but *loses his true identity and misreads objective reality.*

The ignorance operates, and the trance is maintained, by an influence called *maya*, which causes men to misapprehend both natural and supernatural reality—to see it, but to see it as different from what it really is. This is to live literally in illusion, and this is where we all do live. It is in this state that we conduct our philosophy, our science, our education, and our politics; in this state we hope and plan and work, make war and peace, marry and have children, live and die.

The possibility of breaking out of this chain of waking dreams is made more difficult by a further complication. Remember that in the ignorance, in the hypnotic trance of *maya*, God is veiled, my Self is veiled, and objects are veiled. What I experience are images—shadows of real things.

Now at this point my *imagination* takes over, and by its power I take the shadows for reality. I then experience myself as separate and apart from everything else.

This is no fairy story and certainly no joke. In dreadful actuality I am effectively alienated, effectively cut off, effectively separated from

God, from my Self, *and from objective reality.* What I call "objective reality"— and what the world calls "objective reality"—is a play of images. The true reality of everything—not only of God but of every rock and tree—is hidden from me by the ignorance. My actual, effective, daily experience is that of separation and alienation. And it is a hideously false experience.

The terrible circuit is closed by the fact that *I am ignorant of the ignorance.* I do not know, or even suspect, the cause of the human plight, so I bull ahead and commit all kinds of major and minor horrors—calling this "life"—always hoping for better times, which of course never come, or if they do, never stay—not realizing that there can be no better times as long as the ignorance prevails, as long as the trance continues, as long as I take shadows for reality.

The purpose of yoga—in the West as well as in the East, and in all ages and all religions—is to *break the trance,* to awaken from the sleep of ignorance and the nightmares of violence and injustice.

What needs to be joined in yoga? The individual human consciousness—illusorily but hypnotically and effectively separated—needs to be reunited to the reality with which it is essentially and eternally one.

A veil needs to be rent and a spell broken. That is all. But that is everything.

The secret which yoga proposes to penetrate is the secret which holds all mankind in bondage. It is no light enterprise. Again—it is a mistake to begin practice before you have informed yourself of the major contours of the road you are intending to travel.

The question, "How to *practice* yoga?" cannot be answered quickly. You can make a start with some very simple know-how, but the skills involved and the knowledge needed quickly become deeper as you go.

And as you experience the positive power and good results of yoga more and more strongly, in proportion you will begin to encounter the dangers of yoga.

It is sentimental, foolish, and in the highest degree dangerous to pretend that there are no dangers or that they are unimportant. There *are* dangers and they are real and serious.

Yoga is like an automobile: it is an efficient vehicle for a certain kind of traveling; but at the same time, if you use it ignorantly, carelessly, or violently, it can injure or kill you.

How do you learn yoga?

There are two ways: (1) You learn it by studying the literature, applying what you learn in daily practice, and exchanging knowledge with others who are going this way. Or (2) you learn it from a guru, and you practice under the guru's direction.

If you are fortunate enough to have a real guru, you do not need this book, or any literature except such as the guru may prescribe.

The trouble is that a real guru is exceedingly hard to find and for most people impossible to find.

A real guru is not a mere instructor in philosophy, posture, and exercise. There are considerable numbers of people around who

The oldest science on earth undoubtedly is the science of human self-discovery and psycho-physical regeneration called yoga. And the most ancient yogis were not Hindus but Egyptians. Egyptian yoga is unique in that its chief meditative posture is not cross-legged on the ground but seated upon a chair or throne.

The Egyptian posture is well suited to modern men and women who for one reason or another cannot manage the cross-legged postures. The back is kept easily straight, with the neck relaxed and the head "floating" on top of the spine, and with the chin and the gaze level. Palms are placed on the thighs, fingertips at or near the knees. The heels are two to six inches apart, thighs relaxed, legs slightly splayed. The height of the chair should be such that the feet can be placed flat on the ground without putting undue pressure on the bottom of the thighs. The back may be slightly away from the back of the chair or lightly touching it.

This is a sound sacred posture which almost anyone can master in a few months and which is very suitable for prayer, concentration, and meditation.

have practiced yoga for a while and who are capable of teaching the postures and exercises. But these are not gurus.

A real guru is a human being who has himself reached the goal of yoga; who himself is liberated; who knows God and is established in God; through whom God speaks and teaches.

A real guru has the audacity and the power to take full responsibility for the disciple's life, spiritual and physical welfare, progress through the most difficult stages of yoga, and final liberation.

If you can find a real guru, and he will accept you, by all means learn your yoga that way. It is incomparably the best way, and many of the traditional schools insist that it is the only way.

My own experience has been that I hoped for a guru and looked for a guru over a period of many years, but I never came close to finding anything remotely resembling the real article.

I learned posture, exercises, and philosophy from books and from various people who were qualified to share experience in these things, but none of them were gurus and none claimed to be gurus.

There are a few mere posture-teachers who give themselves out as gurus, and in my opinion these constitute one of the serious early dangers of the yogic way. A naive disciple and a bogus guru are a disaster-making combination for both parties. Better—far better—to have no guru at all than to have a phony guru.

The simple fact is that a real guru is such an exceedingly rare item in the modern world that nine hundred ninety-nine out of a thousand people who would gladly find and follow one have absolutely no chance of doing so. If they are going to practice yoga at all, they are going to have to practice without a guru.

But is that possible?

I believe so. That is the way I have learned, and my experience has been, and continues to be, a very good one. I am encouraged by the fact that all of the great traditions say that the authentic human guru is in every case literally the envoy, manifestation, and mouthpiece (*rasulu*) of the one true Guru, who is none other than God himself.

I believe that those who seek union but cannot find a human guru are invariably taught by God himself, and never so much so as in our time. The possibilities in this way for self-deception are great, but they are great in the other way, too—in the present day and age possibly greater.

If you happen to be a Christian yogi, the problem is clarified in notable passages in the scripture; in James: "My brethren, be not many teachers . . ." and in Matthew, (Jesus speaking): "But be ye not called Rabbi; for one is your Master, even Christ, and all ye are brethren. And call no man your father upon the earth; for one is your Father, who is in heaven. Neither be ye called masters: for one is your Master, even Christ."

4

Ramakrishna on Yoga

by John Burns

IF YOU DO NOT YET KNOW Sri Ramakrishna, you have a great experience in store for you. If you do know Ramakrishna, you know what I mean.

I remember my first acquaintance. In 1943 I was poking around in a book store in Grand Central Station during my lunch hour. I was a Madison Avenue advertising writer. I had recently become a member of Alcoholics Anonymous, where I felt much at home and pleased and excited at what was happening to me, but where I heard a lot of talk about God. And I was of two minds about that. One mind said, I am still a staunch atheist and they can take all this God talk and stuff it up the chimney; the other mind said, maybe there is something to it.

Well, in this book store I picked up a book called *The Gospel of Sri Ramakrishna* by M. It turns out that M. is somebody who recorded a lot of conversations with an Indian holy man named Ramakrishna (1836-1886). I opened the book to a place where Ramakrishna is saying that it is possible to see God face to face, just as you see another person, and to talk with him. I thought, "What is this? Is this crazy? Or could it be so?" A door long closed inside my mind opened a crack. If it could be so, wouldn't *that* be something! Quite a difference from the usual arguments. The arguments, really, were what I was sick of. The possibility of experience of God —of an actual conversation with God—this grabbed me. And here was a man who had had such experience. Which made him a nut, or— *what?*

What Ramakrishna is, you may find out by

reading the book. Of course you will not find out anything about this man or any such man if you do not have what Gurdjieff called magnetic center: the innate capacity for responding at least slightly to the truth of the holy life, the sacred path, the Way. (Atheists, incidentally, occasionally have a livelier magnetic center than some "believers.")

Ramakrishna was a man who fulfilled Christ's specification for eternal life: He knew God. And he taught with authority, and not as the scholars.

The Gospel of Sri Ramakrishna is a big book in every way. In thirty-two years of study I have not begun to exhaust it; on the contrary, I return to it again and again and am always finding new strength and new wisdom in it.

Whitman said of his own book, "Who touches this book touches a man." Who touches the Ramakrishna book touches more than a man. To an extraordinary degree the book communicates the power and reality of God, and the Way to God.

The matter of the real status of Ramakrishna, of his being an avatar and an incarnation of God, are questions beyond the scope of this discussion. What does not, however, require any particular erudition or depth or subtlety to see—what must be clear to any but a shut mind—is that Ramakrishna was a man who knew God face to face—who knew the way to God from direct experience and achievement—and who had a *commission from God himself to teach.*

In a conversation with Pundit Shashadhar, one

SRI RAMAKRISHNA

of the renowned Sanskrit scholars of his time and a pillar of orthodox Hinduism, the following exchange took place:

> *Master:* "Tell me how you give your lectures."
> *Pundit:* "Sir, I try to explain the teachings of the Hindu scriptures."
> *Master:* "For the Kaliyuga the path of devotion described by Nārada is best . . ."
>
> The Master continued: "When I first heard about you I inquired whether you were merely erudite or whether you had discrimination and renunciation. A pundit who doesn't know how to discriminate between the Real and the unreal is no pundit at all.
>
> "There is no harm in teaching others if the preacher has a commission from the Lord. Nobody can confound a preacher who teaches people after having received the command of God. Getting a ray of light from the goddess of learning, a man becomes so powerful that before him big scholars seem mere earthworms.
>
> "When the lamp is lighted the moths come in swarms. They don't have to be invited. In the same way, the preacher who has a commission from God need not invite people to hear him. He doesn't have to announce the time of his lectures. He possesses such irresistible attraction that people come to him of their own accord. People of all classes, even kings and aristocrats, gather around him. They say to him: 'Revered sir, what can we offer you? Here are mangoes, sweets, money, shawls, and other things. What will you be pleased to accept?' In that case I say to them: 'Go away. I don't care for these. I don't want anything.'"*

If indeed Ramakrishna had God's commission to teach—and if, as every great teacher has taught, union with God and the things that con-

---

* This quotation and those following are from *The Gospel of Sri Ramakrishna* by M. (pages 245, 464, 465, 466, 467, 468, 499, and 500) and from *Sri Ramakrishna, the Great Master* by Swami Saradananda (pages 159 and 160).

duce to union with God are the only possible sane goals and concerns for a human being—then what Ramakrishna has to say about union, yoga, is of the highest authority and of the utmost importance for anyone seeking God in this time.

The world is now flooded with yogic teaching. Some of it is valid; much of it is half-baked, distorted, and otherwise corrupt; and some of it is demonic. Yoga is a powerful means to the greatest of all ends, but like all powerful things it is dangerous, and you can hurt yourself, nay, you can ruin yourself with it if you do not exercise wisdom. Ramakrishna's teaching on yoga is obviously valid and highly relevant to the conditions and problems of this age. It is particularly helpful in the clear warnings and cautions given against practices which are inappropriate and dangerous, with very few exceptions, for twentieth-century men.

In the same conversation with Pundit Shashadhar, the Master says that it doesn't matter which yogic path you follow. And yet further on he points out that certain practices are very much more suitable today than others:

> (*To the pundit*) "Therefore I say to you, dive into the Ocean of Satchidānanda. Nothing will ever worry you if you but realize God. Then you will get His commission to teach people.
>
> "There are innumerable pathways leading to the Ocean of Immortality. The essential thing is to reach the Ocean. It doesn't matter which path you follow. Imagine that there is a reservoir containing the Elixir of Immortality. You will be immortal if a few drops of the Elixir somehow get into your mouth. You may get into the reservoir either by jumping into it, or by being

pushed into it from behind, or by slowly walking down the steps. The effect is one and the same. You will become immortal by tasting a drop of that Elixir.

"Innumerable are the ways that lead to God. There are the paths of jnāna, of karma, and of bhakti. If you are sincere, you will attain God in the end, whichever path you follow. Roughly speaking, there are three kinds of yoga: jnānayoga, karmayoga, and bhaktiyoga.

"What is jnānayoga? The jnāni seeks to realize Brahman. He discriminates, saying, 'Not this, not this.' He discriminates, saying, 'Brahman is real and the universe illusory.' He discriminates between the Real and the unreal. As he comes to the end of discrimination, he goes into samādhi and attains the Knowledge of Brahman.

"What is karmayoga? Its aim is to fix one's mind on God by means of work. That is what you are teaching. It consists of breath-control, concentration, meditation, and so on, done in a spirit of detachment. If a householder performs his duties in the world in a spirit of detachment, surrendering the results to God and with devotion to God in his heart, he too may be said to practise karmayoga. Further, if a person performs worship, japa, and other forms of devotion, surrendering the results to God, he may be said to practise karmayoga. Attainment of God alone is the aim of karmayoga.

"What is bhaktiyoga? It is to keep the mind on God by chanting His name and glories. For the Kaliyuga the path of devotion is easiest. This is indeed the path for this age."

Ramakrishna said that spiritual consciousness is not possible without the awakening of the Kundalini (the vital fire which lies dormant and coiled at the base of the spine). The awakening of the Kundalini is a very serious and dangerous undertaking. It is a prime objective of yoga, without which there is no spiritual awakening and no samadhi (superconsciousness). One should not ignore the dangers, but neither should one ignore the fact that without awaken-

ing the spinal fire no spiritual experience is possible.

The Master began the conversation by addressing the Bāul musicians from Shibpur.

Master: "Yoga is not possible if the mind dwells on 'woman and gold.' The mind of a worldly man generally moves among the three lower centres: those at the navel, at the sexual organ, and at the organ of evacuation. After great effort and spiritual practice the Kundalini is awakened. According to the yogis there are three nerves in the spinal column: Idā, Pingalā, and Sushumnā. Among the Sushumnā are six lotuses, or centres, the lowest being known as the Mulādhāra. Then come successively Svādhisthāna, Manipura, Anāhata, Visuddha, and Ājnā. These are the six centres. The Kundalini, when awakened, passes through the lower centres and comes to the Anāhata, which is at the heart. It stays there. At that time the mind of the aspirant is withdrawn from the three lower centres. He feels the awakening of Divine Consciousness and sees Light. In mute wonder he sees that radiance and cries out: 'What is this? What is this?'

"After passing through the six centres, the Kundalini reaches the thousand-petalled lotus known as the Sahasrāra, and the aspirant goes into samādhi.

"According to the Vedas these centres are called 'bhumi,' 'planes.' There are seven such planes. The centre at the heart corresponds to the fourth plane of the Vedas. According to the Tantra there is in this centre a lotus called Anāhata, with twelve petals.

"The centre known as Visuddha is the fifth plane. This centre is at the throat and has a lotus with sixteen petals. When the Kundalini reaches this plane, the devotee longs to talk and hear only about God. Conversation on worldly subjects, on 'woman and gold,' cause him great pain. He leaves a place where people talk of these matters.

"Then comes the sixth plane, corresponding to the centre known as Ājnā. This centre is located between the eyebrows and it has a lotus with two petals. When

Ramakrishna said over and over again, "Yoga [union with God] is not possible if the mind dwells on 'woman and gold.'" By "woman and gold" of course he means sex and wealth, the two preoccupations around which worldly life revolves.

Here is a watershed. On this point spiritual seekers fall into two groups: those who go on to real knowledge of God, and those who settle for merely talking about God, allowing sex and wealth to absorb most of their life energies.

Sex and wealth obviously are not evil in themselves; both are God-ordained and good things. But here we have the old dilemma: you cannot serve two masters. If God is to be our Lord and our Lover, we

must give him the same intense, all-consuming devotion that misers give to their money and young lovers give to one another. Such devotion—nothing less—conduces to living experience of the Supreme Reality. And in the nature of things it leaves little time over for preoccupation with "woman and gold."

What often happens, however, is precisely the opposite. Sex and wealth become objects of adoration, displacing love of God and even mere interest in God. With the result that "woman and gold" become deadly obstacles and finally totally effective obstacles to the life of union with God.

the Kundalini reaches it, the aspirant sees the form of God. But still there remains a slight barrier between the devotee and God. It is like a light inside a lantern. You may think you have touched the light, but in reality you cannot because of the barrier of the glass. . . .

"After passing the six centres the aspirant arrives at the seventh plane. Reaching it, the mind merges in Brahman. The individual soul and the Supreme Soul become one. . . . Spiritual consciousness is not possible without the awakening of the Kundalini."

Finally, everyone who seriously practices yoga should take seriously Ramakrishna's warning against trying to make a full *way* of the practices of hathayoga.

Postures and breathing exercises have their place. (Ramakrishna's spiritual heir, Vivekananda, who certainly understood his Master's teaching, has written a definitive book on rajayoga, of which hathayoga is a division.) But if hathayoga is taken as the whole way, without the most competent guidance, disaster is apt to ensue. In this connection Saradananda, a direct disciple of the Master and a major biographer, has written:

He forbade us later to practise the hathayoga exercises, because he himself practised them and knew their results. Approached by some of us for instruction on it, he said to us, "These practises are not for this age. Living beings are shortlived and their lives depend on food in the Kaliyuga; where is the time in this age to practise rajayoga, in other words, to call on God, after making the body firm by the practise of hathayoga? Again, if one wants to practise those exercises, one has to live constantly with a teacher perfect in that yoga and follow for a long time very hard rules regarding food, rest, exercises, etc., according to his instruction; the slightest deviation from those rules produces diseases in the sadhaka's body and, on many occasions, causes even his death.

It would be unfortunate if these warnings were to keep anyone from practicing psychophysical disciplines which are a valid and necessary part of his way to God. *Such exercises do have their place.* But their serious dangers to health and to life itself need the strongest possible emphasis in this age when irresponsibility is the order of the day. Moral: do not practice any but the simplest and most rudimentary psychophysical yogic exercises unless you are sure they are in your svadharma, unless you are sure of competent guidance, and unless you are sure of your own capacity for wisdom and strict obedience. These are very hard things to be sure about.

5

Prerequisites of Yoga

by Thomas R. White

ALL THE TRUTHS of the Way, and the Way of the Grail, are old. You might think this unfortunate, since our culture is so hung up on having everything new.

But when you begin to see the truths of the Way as *true*, when you get hold of the fact that they are not merely outdated opinions of old sages but are the axioms on which the whole universe turns, they come alive. They give meaning and direction to any conceivable situation which a twentieth-century man may happen to find himself in.

You can't get into the Way without breaking out of modern parochial notions of time. *Our Times* are not the past ten years, or fifty years, or hundred years—as the modern mind assumes. Our Times are the past five thousand years. Present-day man is a child of the last five millennia (*not* a very long time but a very *brief* time as earthtime goes). If you narrow your vision down to one per cent of the era into which you are born, you will never get the teaching you need in order to awaken, to arise, to find out who and what you are, and to become regenerate in God—*and anything less than that is a radical life failure.*

You must *not* write off men like Jesus and Muhammad as if they were old-timers. They are very recent, very modern men, sent to teach this modern age. And you must not write off as a Sunday school book character such a man as, for example, the prophet Daniel, whose teaching is remarkably and indeed terrifyingly related to the times of the end, the particular part of the epoch in which we happen to be leading our immediate short earth-lives.

It takes heart to take a man like Daniel seriously, because his stature and power and integrity as a human being tend to dwarf us. We come upon the tremendous records of his life and his teaching with our pathetic little prejudices against the supernatural and against the living reality of God, and when we hear that he stood up for his truth against his temporal ruler's edict and for that was thrown into a den of lions and the lions would not touch him, we fall back upon nervous little speculations that that must be just an old story dreamed up to amuse children or simple-minded pious folk and that things like that don't really happen.

Well, first of all it isn't an old record. It tells of something that took place only about half way through Our Times, only about five hundred years before Christ. (Things that you could properly call old begin before our own age. Something like the submersion of Atlantis, for example, is not very old [ten thousand years, after all, is merely the twinkling of an eye in solar time and a couple of breaths in earth time] but at least it is old in the sense of being outside our particular epoch.)

In the second place things like Daniel in the lions' den *do* happen. They have been happening off and on through all history, and are still happening, with good witnesses testifying to them, right up into the little niche of the past fifty years which we call our own times but which is really only a sliver of our true own times. Men of sanctity, men of truth, men of God develop a peculiar power with regard to

nature and with regard to animals. With or without a special act of grace on God's part, such men are safe among dangerous animals when ordinary men are not. Do you know the record of Brahmananda's encounter with the oncoming angry bull, which he quietly faced, and it turned away? Or the hair-raising account of Sadhu Sundar Singh's midnight meeting with the tiger (witnessed from a window in a nearby house by one of his friends). The Sadhu—a remarkable East Indian Christian—was meditating on a hillside in the moonlight, and a large tiger approached and lay down beside him, remained there for a long time, and finally got up and walked off into the night.

The prophet Daniel was far more truly a man of Our Times than most of us living today. He was a true citizen of this epoch who spoke, as we have said, particularly for the men of this terrible century in which time is running out. The intrinsic value of his prophetic utterances is recognized and exalted by Christ's most solemn references to them.

There is a remarkable thing about Daniel's appearance on the human scene. He is one of a constellation of holy men of the first rank, all of whom were near-contemporaries or actual contemporaries. No such simultaneity in the appearance of major teachers has occurred before or since in human history. Within the span of a single century, in the sixth century before the coming of Messias, there appeared in India the Buddha, in China Lao Tse and Confucius, in the Holy Land the great prophets Daniel, Ezekiel, and Jeremiah, and in Greece the pivotal teachers

Socrates and Pythagoras.

These truly modern men, these giants of Our Times, all speak with one voice; and, with many different intonations and different bases of teaching, all agree in certain simple fundamentals:

Man's spirit is immortal. Man's source and true home is God. Man is inevitably involved in redeeming this corrupt planet. The Way and the means of our redemption is the Truth. How man lives matters desperately because it affects how he dies, and how he dies affects what comes after death. He is to honor parents, love neighbors, cleave to one wife, trust in God.

Most of our role models are men of earlier times and other cultures. There seem nowadays to be many men of learning and insight, but fewer and fewer men of *being*—men whose words and example compel imitation.

One of the evils of ordinary life in all ages is inability to see beyond sect, class, generation, nationality, or race. Gandhi—like Christ, and like other great teachers of all sects, classes, generations, nationalities, and races—stood against this narrowness. He did not deny the real differences. But he insisted that the oneness of Truth, God, to whom all men on the Way everywhere relate, is a deeper reality than the differences. This is the kind of truth great road men help us to see for ourselves.

There are hundreds of men in all the cultures of mankind whose work and lives we can study. Some are saints, like Thomas, Francis, and Ramakrishna. Some are artists like Rembrandt, Beethoven, and Blake. Some are philosophers like Socrates, Plato, Thoreau, and Buber. Some

Help—all help—comes from God. It often comes through natural channels, but it comes from God. This is what the world has forgotten. And this is the beautiful truth which you rediscover when you enter the Way and begin living the life that leads to liberation. Real help is available at all times and all places for the mere asking. This realization alone makes all the difference between a life of weakness and despair and a life of strength and joy.

Drawing by William Blake

are leaders and men of action like Gandhi and Martin Luther King.

The great religions are still otherwise probably the best place to find living teachers. This is not to say that everyone in the great religions—Judaism, Islam, Buddhism, Hinduism, Christianity—can be your teacher. Far from it. It is easy to be "in a religion" but not serious about it. Scattered around, however, are people who are living their religion in desperate truth. Some are priests, ministers, and rabbis; some are ordinary citizens; but they are there, waiting to help you if you will approach. They almost certainly will never appear if you do nothing more about your religion than go perfunctorily to services once a week.

And then there are books. In books—far more broadly and sometimes more effectively than anywhere else—you can share the wisdom of people who have actually travelled long distances and reached very high ground on the Way and who know from experience what it is all about.

All of these teachings and teachers agree on the *first step*: the problem is how to achieve self-mastery. "Master thyself, then others shall thee beare." This was Ezra Pound's conclusion—in pathos—after a lifetime of frantic effort to get the world to listen to his formulas for social change. The formulas won't do it. "Things go on exactly as they have always gone on before." But let some few men achieve self-mastery, let them merely work toward it seriously for a while, and order and calm will begin to form around them like the silence at the center of the hurricane.

In all this we do not think we are talking of anything lofty or spiritually advanced. It is, as Tolstoy wrote, merely the first step. But it is a step Westerners in general, and Western Christians in particular are peculiarly prone to omit. The result is that we build our spiritual houses on sand. We attempt lofty virtues and even imagine we possess them, when in fact our lives are ruled by gluttony, greed, or lust.

> In olden times, when there was no Christian teaching, all the teachers of life, beginning with Socrates, regarded as the first virtue of life, self-control—*engkrateia* or *sophrosune;* and it was understood that every virtue must begin with and pass through this one. It was clear that a man who had no self-control, who had developed an immense number of desires and had yielded himself up to them, could not lead a good life. It was evident that before a man could even think of disinterestedness, justice—to say nothing of generosity or love—he must learn to exercise control over himself. According to our ideas now, nothing of the sort is necessary. We are convinced that a man who has developed his desires to the climax reached in our society, a man who cannot live without satisfying the hundred unnecessary habits that enslave him, can yet lead an altogether moral and good life.
>
> *The First Step*, Leo Tolstoy

Why do most of us refuse to take the first stages of the spiritual life (what Tolstoy calls the good life) seriously, while we so love to claim that we seek God, help our neighbor, and are dedicated to "higher values"?

We simply do not believe that what the ancients called self-control (moderation), or what Christianity calls self-renunciation is strictly necessary. We are hung up in a lunatic expectation that we can lead good lives while continuing to lead obviously evil ones. Tolstoy's view of the situation is remarkably incisive and applicable today. It is worth quoting at some length:

> . . . A man who believes that there are means other than personal effort by which he may escape sin or its results, cannot strive with the same energy and seriousness as the man who knows no other means. And not striving with perfect seriousness, and knowing of other means besides personal effort, a man will inevitably neglect the unalterable order of succession for the attainment of the good qualities necessary to a good life. And this has happened with the majority of those who profess Christianity. . . .
>
> The great mass of those who accepted Christianity, accepting it only externally, took advantage of the substitution of Christianity for paganism to rid themselves of the demands of the heathen virtues—no longer necessary for a Christian—and to free themselves from all conflict with their animal nature.
>
> The same thing happens with those who cease to believe in the teaching of the Church. They . . . put forward some imaginary good work, approved of by the majority of men, such as the service of science, art, or humanity; and in the name of this imaginary good work they liberate themselves from the consecutive attainment of the qualities necessary for a good life, and are satisfied, like men on the stage, with pretending to live a good life.
>
> Those who fell away from paganism without embracing Christianity in its true significance, began to preach love for God and man apart from self-renunciation, and justice without self-control; that is to say, they preached the higher virtues omitting the lower ones: i.e., not the virtues themselves, but the semblance.
>
> Some preach love to God and man without self-renunciation, and others humaneness, the service of humanity, without self-control. And as this teaching,

while pretending to introduce man into higher moral regions, encourages his animal nature by liberating him from the most elementary demands of morality—long ago acknowledged by the heathens, and not only rejected but strengthened by true Christianity—it was readily accepted both by believers and unbelievers.

Tolstoy thus nailed down the remarkable way that we have succeeded in watering down and distorting Christ's teachings, making them, in the end, less challenging to our ordinary, run-of-the-mill viciousness than honest paganism would have been. It is no wonder, as Tolstoy himself observed, that his arguments were everywhere received with a "cold and hostile silence."

It was Santayana who said somewhere that we Americans are slow to realize that number and extension have nothing to do with quality. Put it another way: the fact that a lot of people do something, or do not do something, does not prove a thing about whether it is right or wrong. Quality comes from the truth. The truth is the truth whether one man believes it and no others, or even if no men believe it. Meister Eckhart said that if God could somehow backslide from the truth, he would let God go and stick with the truth.

6

Surya Namaskars

by Henry Woods

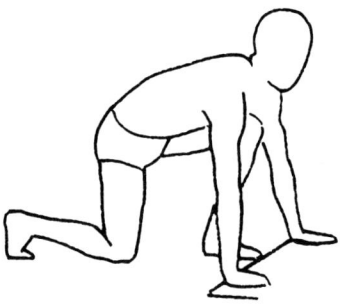

DISCIPLINED POSTURE and breathing as a base for prayer and meditation—raja yoga—has powerfully beneficial effects from a purely physiological standpoint. It develops suppleness and conscious control over the physical organism as nothing else will. It also produces some isotonic effect, that is to say it involves enough contraction of the skeletal muscles to increase overall muscle strength and tone—up to a point.

But working with yogic postures (*asanas*) will not by itself keep you in top physical condition. Raja yoga, no matter how extended or intensive, has virtually no aerobic value. It will not strengthen the cardiovascular system, and it will not build endurance. Another kind of training is essential to balance your development. Aerobic exercise, which increases the efficiency with which the body processes oxygen, is necessary to good health.

If the practice of *asanas* will not produce an aerobic effect, what will? Some people take up jogging or bike riding, and those are adequate ways to condition aerobically, but they provide none of the benefits of yogic training. There is, however, a better way—a *yogic exercise* which has *high aerobic value* and at the same time produces the suppleness, body-control, and isotonic benefits that *asanas* do. Nothing we know of comes anywhere near, for ease, thoroughness, and general good results, to a system of exercises called Surya Namaskars.

These may very well be the best setting-up exercises in the world. Taken by themselves and done in sufficient quantity, they are a virtually self-sufficient scheme for getting and maintaining a high level of physical fitness. In moderate amounts, Surya Namaskars are a superb introduction to each day's raja yoga session.

Surya Namaskars (literal translation: Sun Prayers) are an old form of exercise and worship combined. They come out of the yogic practice of ancient India. They were introduced to the West about thirty years ago by a remarkable man, the then Rajah of Aundh (a small state near Bombay), who wrote a book about them: *The Ten-Point Way to Health.* *

Just about anybody who does not have a special health problem can do Namaskars. You can do them in a two foot by seven foot space right in your own bedroom. And they only take five to twenty minutes a day, depending on how many you do.

Each Namaskar combines ten different positions with three controlled breaths. The drawings presented here are carefully done to indicate exactly what each position should look like. Note especially the breath indicators which show you how to relate breathing to the positions. In changing from position to position, strive to go as smoothly as possible. An overall feeling of fluidity should be your goal.

Do your Namaskars in a minimum of clothing—underwear or a bathing suit. To begin, spread a cloth about two feet square on the floor. A towel will do.

---

* *The Ten-Point Way to Health,* Surya Namaskars, by Shrimant Balasahib Pandit Pratinidhi, B.A., Rajah of Aundh, edited with an introduction by Louise Morgan (New York, 1939: David Kemp Company).

Position One.* Stand upright with your feet and knees together and your toes touching the edge of the towel. Place your hands on your chest, palms together. Stand tall. Consciously try to extend your spine. Look straight ahead. Now press your palms firmly together and stiffen your whole body. At the same time, inhale (Breath One), and hold.

Position Two. Keeping your knees straight, drop your hands to the floor, placing the palms on the towel just within the edge, with the fingers together, pointing into the towel. At the same time, exhale completely.

If you find yourself unable, with your knees held straight, to get your fingers to the ground, much less your palms, do not be discouraged. This is standard experience for the not-so-supple and in no way interferes with the good you can derive from Namaskars. Just go down as far as you can without straining. In all of the positions, approximations are completely valid to begin with. You will be amazed at how quickly you improve.

Position Three. From this position until Position Nine your hands remain fixed on the towel, and are your "pivot." Inhale (Breath Two) and hold. Without bending your arms, drop your right knee to the ground, parallel to and somewhat behind your left foot. Lift your head as high as you can, looking upward. Your right knee and toes should be touching the ground. Your left thigh should be pressed against the left side of your chest and stomach. Your left knee should stick out slightly ahead of the still-vertical left

---

* See picture sequence beginning on the following page.

2

Exhale

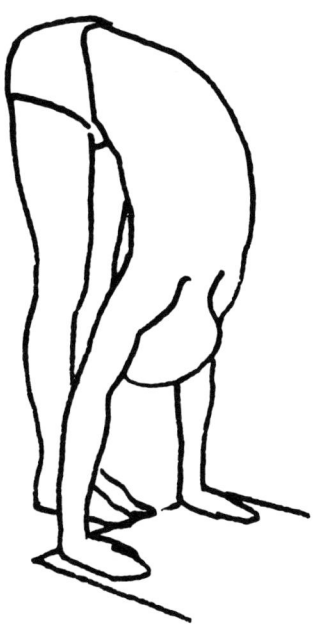

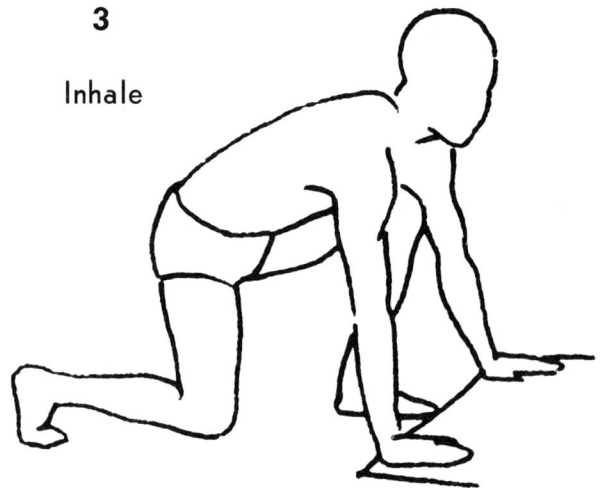

5

Exhale

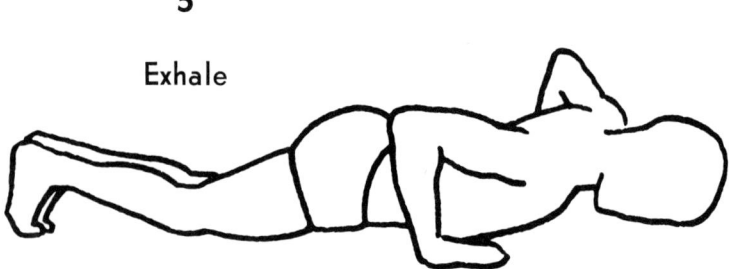

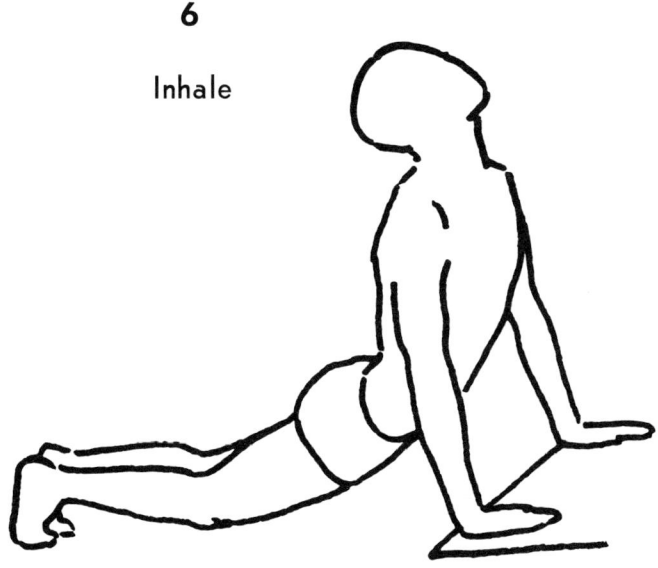

6

Inhale

7

Hold Breath

8

Hold Breath

9

Exhale

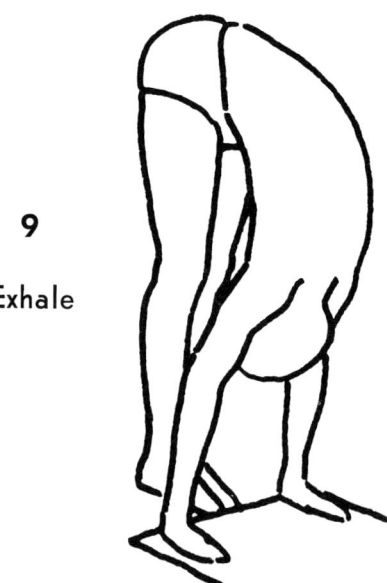

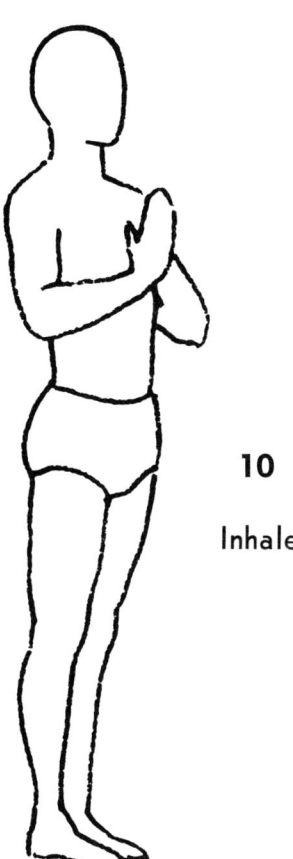

10

Inhale

arm. Your left foot should remain unmoved, flat on the ground, toes touching the edge of the towel.

Position Four. Keep holding your breath. Keep your hands and arms as in Position Three. Raise your body, and push your left leg (the "up" knee in Position Three) back to join the right leg. Drop your head.

You should now look like an upside-down V. Your head and neck should be in line with your arms. You will feel pressure on the backs of your knees and ankles if you have assumed the position correctly. Eventually you will be limber enough to have your heels flat on the ground in Position Four, but here, especially, do not force things prematurely, or you may injure yourself.

Position Five. Keeping your hands in place, drop flat on the floor, touching your forehead, nose, chest, knees, and toes, but not your hips or abdomen. Exhale (Breath Two) while you are dropping into Position Five, pushing the last bit of air out of your lungs as you draw your abdomen up and in.

Position Six. Your hands, toes, and knees remain as in Position Five. Straighten your arms. Inhale (Breath Three). Throw your chest out as far as possible. Curve your back, and look at the ceiling, stretching your neck back as far as possible. (This is a variant of the raja yoga posture called the cobra.)

Hold Breath Three through Positions Seven and Eight. Let it out in Position Nine. Rising from Position Nine to Position Ten, you inhale the next breath, which is Breath One of the next Namaskar (unless you decide to rest for one breath or several between Namaskars).

Beginning with Position Seven, you complete the Namaskar by repeating Positions One through Four in reverse order:

>Position Seven = Position Four
>Position Eight = Position Three
>Position Nine = Position Two
>Position Ten = Position One

Position Seven. Get back up into the inverted V posture.

Position Eight. Drop down on your knee. This time go down on your left knee instead of the right knee as you did in Position Three. The reason for this slight variation is simply to produce an alternating and balancing effect. In Position Eight your left knee and toes should be touching the ground. Your right thigh should be pressed against the right side of your chest and stomach. Your arms should be vertical, palms down on the towel. Your head should be lifted, eyes looking upward.

Position Nine. Keep your palms on the towel. Stand up and put your feet together, toes touching the edge of the towel. Your legs should be as near straight as possible. You should be bent over at the waist, your face in close to your knees.

Position Ten. Straighten up from the waist, bringing your hands to rest on your chest, palms together, as you were positioned at the beginning of the Namaskar.

Memorizing the breaths and positions takes a bit of doing. But after just a few practice sessions, you will find them all fitting beautifully into a smooth cycle.

Warning—especially to impatient types like myself: Go slow at first. Just one or two Namaskars a day. Impatience is chastised painfully in this game. I have suffered through the sad learning process of doing a couple of Namaskars, feeling invigorated and not at all tired, saying to myself in my euphoria, "There's nothing to this; I'll just rip off eight or ten more," and waking next morning with a set of exquisitely strained tendons, ligaments, and muscles.

Once you have made the decision to begin a program of Namaskars, keep reminding yourself that the tortoise really did win his race with the hare. You will get results *quicker* if you take it easy in the early going.

After a couple of weeks, when you have the cycle down pat and are pretty well loosened up, you should be able to do a Namaskar in forty-five seconds, a series of twelve in nine or ten minutes. The Rajah of Aundh thinks you should do better than that. He says fifteen Namaskars in five minutes for beginners, forty Namaskars in ten minutes by the end of six months. But I think the Rajah is somewhat optimistic. Himself an astounding model of health, he has some difficulty toning his message down for those of us (including us ex-athletes of thirty-five and under) who are in poor enough condition to qualify as near-invalids.

In fairness to the Rajah I should quote what he himself has to say about getting started:

> One should . . . exercise only within the limit of one's strength. Be careful at the beginning, and add gradually

> to the length of the exercise period as one's strength increases. . . .
>
> Above all, do not be in a hurry. Take your ten minutes a day without fail [regardless of how many or how well you do]. . . . Know that if you persist, seeming miracles will happen to you.

Another common tendency to guard against is easy discouragement, easy quitting. This seems to be the opposite of premature forcing, but actually the two are flip sides of a single coin. The same people who simply cannot be restrained from tearing headlong into every new program, are those who never stick to any of them long enough to get any real result.

Virtually all of us suffer from this attitude to a greater or lesser degree. Here is the Rajah on the point:

> A certain amount of discouragement is inevitable at the beginning of all reconstructive systems of physical culture. That period must be lived through perseveringly if success is to be won. But if you will only stick to it, you will feel so full of new hope in a month's time that you will never want to give up the exercises that have bestowed this new life upon you.

Once you are in condition, how many Namaskars should you do each day? Again, my reading is more conservative than the Rajah's. He feels that a mature person in good health can do up to three hundred a day. I have been doing Namaskars for sixteen years. During that time I have been in direct personal contact with fifty or sixty other people who were doing them. None of us has ever done more than forty Namaskars a day on a regular basis. If you worked up higher than that, the results might be terrific, but I cannot say, either from personal experience or direct observation.

I can tell you that I have friends and relatives who for reasons of age or health can do no more than five Namaskars a day. These people feel strongly that they are getting good results from even such a small number. And I can guarantee that twelve Namaskars done every day will strikingly improve your physical and mental state. Twenty will make an even greater difference. And by the time you are doing thirty to forty Namaskars every day—I have done this many over the years—you will find yourself hooked into a real spiritual, mental, and physical power-transformer.

Here are just some of the benefits which the Rajah says that Namaskars will yield:

> They strengthen the entire digestive system and cure or prevent constipation.
> They develop the lungs and prevent tuberculosis, and will help to heal it to a great degree.
> They invigorate the heart, and will remedy high blood pressure, palpitations, and other derangements by improving the circulation of the blood....
> They tone up the nervous system....
> They stimulate glandular activity and give a new vigor to the glands....
> They improve the color and function of the skin....
> They strengthen the neck, shoulders, arms, wrists, fingers, back, waist, abdomen, thighs, knees, calves, and ankles....
> They reduce redundant fat, especially the fat about the abdomen, hips, thighs, neck, and chin.
> They destroy the offensive odor of perspiration.

The Rajah devotes a chapter to the value of Namaskars for women. Since Namaskars take so little time, they are made to order for busy mothers and housewives, not to mention career women. And because they can be done in private, they particularly appeal to women who are reluctant to exercise in public.

The Rajah recommends that women discontinue Namaskars during the menstrual period and during the fifth through nine months of a pregnancy. But otherwise he stresses that they are every bit as beneficial for women as men, and in particular:

> They stimulate the uterus and ovaries; remove menstrual disorders and consequent pain and misery; render childbearing less painful and less dangerous.

At first sight, the Rajah's claims—for both sexes—may seem excessive, but my own experience indicates they are not. I have found that Namaskars are a truly amazing exercise—far more beneficial over the long haul than merely reading about them would ever lead you to suppose.

I first tried doing Namaskars at the age of sixteen. I got very enthusiastic about them right away. In no time I was doing twenty to thirty a day.

I had for years been a chronic cold-catcher and was generally sickly. My sinuses cleared noticeably. I had sharply improved stamina and agility. I began to achieve in athletics in ways I had given up hoping I could. And—less tangible but most memorable of all—Namaskars gave me a greatly enhanced sense of well-being and self-confidence.

For many years I continued to do my Namaskars faithfully. Then I injured my back in an athletic accident.

I never did get back to doing Namaskars as regularly as I had before the accident. I cannot remember why that was. Just one of those occasions when one lets something good slip away.

About two years ago I got interested in raja yoga. I underwent training in that discipline which then became the focus for my psychophysical activity, until quite recently. when a serious illness interfered with all efforts to keep some exercise going.

Then I remembered the Namaskars. I did not dare to be too hopeful. I was afraid that they might produce an aggravation of my weakness as did the raja yoga postures to which they are so closely related.

I tried one Namaskar. No problem. Then I tried three. Still okay. I have now worked up to twenty-five a day. I do twenty in the morning for a basic workout and five at bedtime to relax and help me get to sleep. I am experiencing the same surge of good feelings that I did sixteen years ago when I first took up Namaskars. I can do more work on less sleep than at any time in the past nine months. I feel as if I had discovered the fountain of youth. I keep asking myself how I could ever have drifted away from the daily practice of Namaskars.

And now for the last, supremely important point about Namaskars. I hope that by my ending with this aspect of them, you will be sure not to forget or minimize it.

Surya Namaskars means Sun *Prayers*. They involve the whole man. You are not doing the whole Namaskar if you do the positions without breathing properly. And the breathing and positions together are incomplete unless combined with meditation. The Rajah accompanied his Namaskars with Hindu mantras—the repetition of sacred syllables. I combine mine with repetitive prayer in the name of Jesus.

Every time I inhale I say, "Lord Jesus Christ." When I am holding a breath I say, "Son of God." And when I exhale I say, "Have mercy on me." In this fashion I repeat a prayer containing the saving name of Jesus three times in the course of each Namaskar. The joy and power from Namaskars depend even more on my concentration on this meditation than on the sheerly physical aspect.

You can select a prayer to accompany Namaskars that fits your own conception of a Power greater than yourself. But do be sure to round out your practice of them with this meditative element.

Unless you have some insuperable philosophical difficulty on the point, I urge that you not neglect or undervalue the suggestion that you build the meditation which accompanies your Namaskars specifically around repeated prayer in the name of Jesus Christ. The invocation of Messias does something very special— something much bigger than I properly appreciated or understood until I had been at it for some years. It fuses these Eastern yogic exercises with the most powerful of Christian mantras and transforms Namaskars into true *Grail Yoga*—a unitive development of all the physical centers wedded to a communion with the Eternal Word of God, the Fountainhead of all health, joy, and harmony, the Divine Hypostis who became man for the salvation of all men—young and old—male and female—Eastern and Western.

The split between body and spirit is an illusion, a figure of speech. It does not exist. Body and spirit are parts of a whole being. Any effort to work on one while ignoring the other is unbalanced and incomplete. The beauty of the system of Surya Namaskars is that it is a total discipline, one which stimulates awareness of the integration of body and spirit, and produces a transcendent consciousness of unity—that unity which is both the aim and the definition of yoga.

Whether you decide to use Namaskars as a stepping stone into the more advanced disciplines of raja yoga, or as a yoga in themselves, you are in for a powerful experience of exaltation, peace, and strength. I greet you at the start of a most rewarding journey.

24

The Magazine of Living the Way
—Twenty-four Hours at a Time

The Way of the Grail is the search for God—the quest destined for every man, and the whole human race—the universal spiritual journey. *24* is the magazine of pursuing the Way—twenty-four hours at a time. Edited by the editors of Grail Books and Strength Books. Published quarterly. For subscription information, write *24 Magazine,* Hankins, N.Y. 12741.

The great teachings of the whole world have one theme in common. The record of Moses leading his people through the wilderness—Krishna and Arjuna on the field of Kurukshetra—the quest of the knights of the Round Table—these are sublime paradigms of the universal quest for God. *24 Magazine* brings together the great unifying practices of Grail Yoga—the esoteric truths of East and West—esoteric philosophy and history, esoteric literature and science, esoteric art and religion—to show that from the beginning of time until now there has been only one Way, one Tao, one path of truth, one science of regeneration that returns men to spiritual *and physical* reunion with

God. In beautifully illustrated articles *24 Magazine* celebrates both the unity of the Way, as the dominant theme of all history, and its splendid diversity as expressed in the lives of the greatest men and women who ever lived.

24 Magazine is concerned with the day-to-day application of the universal principles of the Way in our own time and to our individual lives. Practically speaking, the Way is a method, a program, a means, and a power for achieving a definite result: a radical change (metanoia) in human consciousness and human nature, bringing with it freedom from want and fear, regeneration of the whole person, and the true brotherhood of man. It is no small thing, but small and weak people can do it, indeed are peculiarly qualified to do it.

The Way is not a religion, but all real religion springs from it—not a science; but all real science obeys its principles—not an art, but all real art is a communication of it. The Way is the power which keeps the stars in their courses, and shows men how to live. It is the way the universe works, and it is the way *you* work when you are in your right mind. It is the Norm of human life. People are sane when they obey it, and insane when they ignore it.

The Way is what the rationalists call the First Principles of Practical Reason and the faithful call the Kingdom of Heaven. All things are made by it, supported by it, and received by it at death. The Way is the Life (Zoe). It is the Law (Torah) and the Presence (Shekinah), the Road (Tariqa) and the Struggle (Akbar), the Path (Tao) and its Power (Teh), the Pattern (Rita) and the Method (Dharma). It is Logos-Sophia, Atman, the ruling Power of the universe in its aspect of illuminator and guide of the human race. It is the Truth, the ultimate Reality, the Self-existent, the Suchness—Aletheia, Sat, al-Haqq, Aehyeh, Tathata. It is Christ, God himself as teacher, helper, friend and savior of men. It is the King of kings and Lord of lords, the blessed and only Potentate. It is all this at one and the same time. And whether you like it or not, or believe it or not, you are dealing with it—positively or negatively—every hour of your life.

WINTER 1975-76

24

The Magazine of Living the Way
—Twenty-four Hours at a Time

Laboratory

A community of sixty-four men, women, and children—a laboratory in the living of the Way to God, twenty-four hours at a time—pursues its work on an east ridge of one of the Western Catskills in a remote part of New York State.

Page 2

The Way of the Grail is the search for God—the quest destined for every man, and the whole human race—the universal spiritual journey. 24 is the journal of pursuing the Way—24 hours at a time.

GRAIL BOOKS are books of the Way of the Grail, the universal search for God—including Esoteric Religion, Esoteric Psychology, Esoteric Philosophy, Esoteric History, Esoteric Science. *Esoteric* means *inner* or *interior*—and hence: *real*, not merely speculative; *universal*, not sectarian; *sacred*, not profane; *for serious seekers*, not for dilettantes.

STRENGTH BOOKS are books about spiritual experience, prayer and meditation, mental and physical health, nutrition, exercise, medicine, and the whole subject of fitness to better qualify us for God's service.

*Grail Books and Strength Books Are
Divisions of East Ridge Press*

Ready Now

SACRED SEX, Thomas R. White, ed. A unique summary of the esoteric truths of true *Tantra*, which is no mere oriental curiosity but *the* way to God for married men and women, Western or Eastern, in this age. 120 pp. 4¼ x7 Profusely illus.
LC 74-84538   ISBN: 0-914896-01-6
Paperbd. **$1.95**

Ready Now

THE WAY TO HIGHER CONSCIOUSNESS, Meredith Murray, ed. A map of the levels of consciousness, from sleep to illumination. A practical guide to the place in ourselves which is our blessed homeland. 136 pp. 4¼ x7 Profusely illus.
LC 74-16879   ISBN: 0-914896-09-1
Paperbd. **$2.50**

Ready Now

WHY DO MEN STUPEFY THEMSELVES? and other writings by **Leo Tolstoy.** Surgical probing by the great Russian of three prime trouble spots in modern life: drugs, fake Christianity, and middle class idleness and self-indulgence. 168 pp. 4¼ x7 Profusely illus.
LC 74-16880   ISBN: 0-914896-08-3
Paperbd. **$2.50**

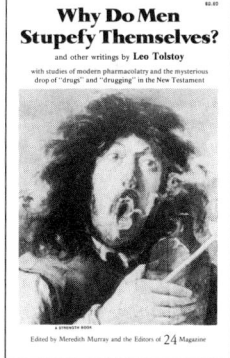

Ready Now

THE GOD-ILLUMINATED COOK, a new presentation of *The Practice of the Presence of God*, by **Brother Lawrence.** This small book is a powerhouse. It can open up a path for you to spiritual enrichment and meaning in life. It has been doing this for God-seeking men and women for over three hundred years. The method is time-tested, the endorsements beyond number.

The man responsible for it was a clumsy French peasant who was admitted as a lay brother among the bare-footed Carmelite monks in Paris in 1666 and became their cook. There among his pots and pans he developed his "practice of the presence of God," the final stage of which is sustained awareness of God, a sense of being upheld and guided by an ever-present Power. Almost accidentally—"providentially" may be the better word—Brother Lawrence's conversations and correspondence on the practical search for God in one's own life were preserved. As the Introduction to this new edition says, "The practice of the presence of God can be done anywhere by anyone who is not dead, crazy, or asleep." Furthermore, although Brother Lawrence offers no Six Easy Lessons with a Money-back Guarantee of Success, his discipline works.

What is the practice? How do you do it? You can find out by reading this book.

144 pp. 4¼ x 7 Profusely illus. LC 74-84399 ISBN: 0-914896-00-8 Paperbd. **$2.50**

Ready Now

TRAINING FOR THE LIFE OF THE SPIRIT, Gerald Heard. Here one of the great thinkers of the twentieth century presents in simple terms the idea that man has a way out of the present chaos through a *further evolution of his consciousness.*

Gerald Heard provides the basic concepts, the points of attack, the regimen, and the vision for undertaking training for continued growth in awareness, understanding, and grasp of Reality. It is these goals that comprise the Life of the Spirit. This is above everything a practical book. Heard's comments on the theory of spiritual life are incisive and profound, but theory is not his main emphasis; he intends to lead his readers to actual experience of higher consciousness. First, he says, *conduct* must be corrected; then *character* must be set right. But these first two steps on the Way serve only to make possible the third: the opening of *consciousness* onto the uplands where contact with the Supreme Reality disperses all doubt. This book is an exploration at great depth by a man who spent a long lifetime in dedicated and brilliantly successful practice of this science of the spirit.

192 pp. 4¼x7 Illus. LC 74-29127 ISBN: 0-914896-11-3   Paperbd. **$2.50**

Coming in Spring, 1976

ALCOHOLICS ANONYMOUS: LIFELINE, John Burns. If you are struggling in the heavy seas of modern life, this book offers a real lifeline and shows you how to get hold of it. You know that Alcoholics Anonymous has sobered up hundreds of thousands of problem drinkers. The reason for AA's success is its Twelve Step recovery program. Yet even within AA few suspect the power of the Twelve Steps to transform *any* troubled life —non-alcoholic as well as alcoholic.

Alcoholics Anonymous: Lifeline is an inside account, written by AA members who themselves recovered as a result of practicing the Steps, and then went on to help in the recoveries of thousands of alcoholics *and others*—including drug addicts, sex addicts, depressives, anxiety freaks, suicidals, psychopaths, and "normapaths."

The Twelve Steps are a unique phenomenon in our age—a practical set of guidelines for the actual attainment of spiritual awakening and conscious contact with God. Their peculiar genius is that they do not require special skill or learning; they work for people in all degrees of mental, emotional, and spiritual disability.

Alcoholics Anonymous: Lifeline tells how the founders of AA put the Steps together. It probes the spiritual depths beneath the surface simplicity of the Steps. And it shows how folks like you and me—whatever our life situation—can practice the Steps to achieve a peace and wholeness rarely found in our time.

168 pp.   4¼ x 7   LC 75-15022   ISBN: 0-914896-27-X   Paperbd. **$2.95**

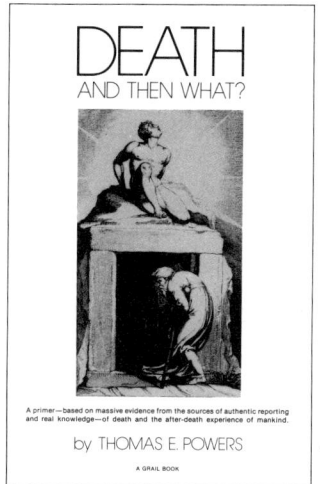

Coming in Spring, 1976

DEATH AND THEN WHAT?, Thomas E. Powers. The materialistic method of dealing with the fact of death is to forget it until you are overtaken by it. The only thing wrong with this plausible prescription is that it does not work. Indeed, it works in reverse. When the terrible mystery of death is processed by nothing more reliable than man's ignoring apparatus, it is merely driven uneasily and shallowly underground. What would be normal fear of death becomes a hell of echoing terrors.

Death and Then What? is a primer of the universal sacred prescription for dealing with death—from which the materialistic view is a 180-degree deviation. The sacred way is to face the fact of death, get your beliefs about death straightened out, and not to forget but deliberately remember death.

For modern men and women, getting your beliefs straightened out is a real workout, because of the fog which the atheistic "enlightenment" of the past several centuries has cast over the whole subject. Death and Then What? gives major attention to the fact that there is no evidence—only a mass of materialistic superstition—that the human being ceases at death. There is on the other hand a huge body of evidence—ancient and modern, traditional and scientific—that death simply releases the living person into another mode and manifold of vital existence. Death and Then What? is concerned with sources of authentic reporting and real knowledge of death and the after-death experience of mankind. With illustrations by Rembrandt, Goya, William Blake, Gustave Moreau, and many others.

120 pp. 5-3/8x8-1/2 Profusely illus. LC 74-16886 ISBN: 0-914896-03-2
                                                    Paperbd. **$2.95**

Coming in Summer, 1976

BREAKTHROUGH TO GOD: THE ULTIMATE EXPERIMENT, Thomas E. Powers. "I first met the author of this book in 1968. At that time I was floating in a certain wonder-struck space which I now see accompanies the first deep experience of the nearness of God. I was visiting my parents, and one day my father brought a friend by to check me out (as I later learned), and determine if I was crazy or not. His name was Tom Powers. He had on a business suit and he could have been your Rotary Club president. The encounter was amazing. Within minutes, there we were, acid-freak, flower-child mystic and urbane advertising executive, engaged, to the wonder of my folks, in an intimate discussion of the secret teaching and starry fields of the pathways to God.

"Now here was one special man. It was obvious that he was wonder-struck too—and at the same time was touching some deep source of practical wisdom. I think what moved me most was the way he combined a vast, unshakable knowledge and faith with a dizzying openness to new ideas. It was completely scientific in its urgency towards the truth.

"It is rare when a book expresses a man's insights as well as this. Distilled here in his step-by-step common sense way are the loftiest ideas of the human race.

"C.P. Snow, I think, was once asked, if he was stuck on a desert island with only one book, what would he pick? His sensible choice was the Boy Scout Handbook. Well, if I were to recommend one book for someone stuck in a disintegrating culture swerving between insatiable materialism or bizarre occultism—it might well be this one. This is one of those rare 'escape manuals' which are suitable both for one who has not yet considered the spiritual quest, and for the most seasoned researcher into this ultimate experiment."—Michael Green.

When this extraordinary testament and work manual first appeared (under the title *First Questions on the Life of the Spirit*), Louis Cassels of United Press International wrote of it: "For those who are already tentatively or securely committed to a religious faith, this book offers a guide toward a deeper understanding of the spiritual life. For those who do not believe in God, but who are troubled by what G.K. Chesterton called 'the first wild doubts of doubt,' it is a compelling invitation to a great experiment."

In the preface to this new edition, Powers writes: "'Experiment' is the keynote of our entire cultural epoch. We have not been content to take anything on hearsay or traditional authority but have wanted to try everything out for ourselves. We have experimented with everything within range of the human mind. With one exception. We have made no experiment upon God. The omission is striking. We have scientifically tested every imaginable datum, except the most elementary, most obvious, and most inescapable datum of all. Why? I think we do not seek God experimentally, scientifically, without fear or favor *because we are afraid of what the result might be.* It might turn out that God is real after all—and the discovery of him would unhinge our world."

Breakthrough to God has played a remarkable part in the growth of groups of spiritual seekers throughout the country who have used it as a basis for their study and experimental work. It is a clear, concise, step-by-step workbook for men and women who are awake both to the futilities and to the unusual opportunities of our times and who are looking for a practical path to spiritual regeneration.

336 pp. 5¼x8¼ Biblio. LC-74-16887 ISBN: 0-914896-02-4   Paperbd. **$4.95**

Grail Books are not only written and/or edited but also designed, set in type, and printed by the same community of Wayfarers who produce *24 Magazine*. This volume is set in 11 point Oracle type on the Compuwriter, and printed on 60-pound Hamilton Vellum Opaque paper, on a Solna 125 offset press.